ADVENTURES IN RECONCILIATION

ADVENTURES IN RECONCILIATION

TWENTY-NINE CATHOLIC TESTIMONIES

edited by

Paddy Monaghan & Eugene Boyle

eagle

Guildford, Surrey

British Library Cataloguing in Publication Data. A catalogue record for this book is available from the British Library.

Typeset by Eagle Publishing
Printed by Cox & Wyman

ISBN No: 0 86347 215 X

To all those courageous Christians who are
building bridges of reconciliation across
denominations and all other divides both
in Ireland and throughout the world.

Acknowledgements

With grateful thanks to the European Programme for
Peace and Reconciliation for funding Eugene Boyle and
Paddy Monaghan in their work for reconciliation in
Ireland.

Many thanks to the brave friends who shared their
testimonies in this book, and to our other friends who
also contributed their testimonies, but space did not
allow them to be included.

Finally, sincere thanks to the six church leaders who
took time out of their busy schedules to contribute to this
project.

CONTENTS

COMMENDATION BY
ARCHBISHOP SEAN BRADY

Archbishop of Armagh and Primate of All Ireland

Adventures in Reconciliation is a rich store of the faith and relationship with the Lord Jesus contained in the testimonies of various people from within the Catholic Church. It is hoped that within their testimonies to the power of God at work in their lives, that we may be helped to see more clearly our own journey with the Lord. That we may be more aware of his guiding, protecting and loving hand touching our daily lives, and that we may hear ever clearer his Word and live this Word more fully day by day. This book is an inspiration to all who wish to follow Christ and grow in love of him.

PREFACE

CARDINAL CAHAL B. DALY

Archbishop Emeritus of Armagh

I have to begin by confessing that, by instinct and formation, I am inclined to be 'allergic' to some of the language
and some of the manifestations of the Evangelical tradition. Maynooth, where I had my seminary formation,
was inclined, in my time, to attach more importance to
the intellectual approach to Christian truths and to dep-
recate what it saw as the 'experiential' element in
religion, which it tended to regard as emotional or sentimental and as prone to excess. Something of that formation remains with me, although I can now see that the
Maynooth tradition in this regard was itself one-sided
and was too cerebral and too intellectualistic. In this
respect, Maynooth was not too untypical of Roman
Catholic Church attitudes in general at that time.

It was partially because of this tradition that the great
flowering of the Charismatic Renewal Movement in the
wake of the Second Vatican Council was received with
some scepticism by many Roman Catholic clergy and
laity at the time. Cardinal Suenens of Malines-Brussels
was one of the first advocates and strongest supporters
of the Renewal Movement. His speech at the Vatican
Council on charisms, or gifts of the Spirit, in the Church
marked a decisive moment in this connection. The
Renewal Movement came to dominate the last twenty or
more years of Cardinal Suenens' long life.

In retrospect, the Renewal Movement has proved to
be a great grace for many within the Roman Catholic

Church. It has given to many Catholics a new love for
and familiarity with Holy Scripture, a newly-felt personal experience of Jesus Christ as their Lord and Saviour, a
new experience of the presence and power of the Holy
Spirit in the Church and in their personal lives. It has
been for many a new experience of spontaneous prayer,
of community prayer, indeed of the sense of Church-as-
community. All this is positive and good. For all this we
Catholics must sincerely thank and praise the Lord.

While personally not feeling 'at ease' with some of the
overt expressions of these experiences, I do affirm that
the experiences themselves and the underlying realities
which are their content are fundamental elements of
Christian and Catholic faith and life. I can claim to be like
Cardinal Newman at least in this (although here, sadly
for me, the likeness ends!) that I have never been able to
separate the experience of the Lord Jesus Christ as my
personal Lord and Saviour from experience of and life in
the visible Church; or to separate experience of the presence and power of the Spirit in my own life from the
experience of the Spirit in the life of the Church; or to
distinguish between 'baptism in the Spirit' and growing
awareness of the reality and power of sacramental baptism and of its implications for my personal life. I believe
that the grace of Christ, given to me in baptism, is continually unfolding itself and empowering Christian
living as 'obedience of faith' to God's Word and God's
call; and this for me is a daily-renewed baptism in the
Spirit. In that connection, I like the *Good News for Modern
Man* translation of 2 Peter 1:10:

> Try even harder to make God's call and his choice of
> you a permanent experience.

For me, as for the late Cardinal Suenens, the 'charismatic' and the 'institutional' Church are one, the Church of
the Spirit and the visible or 'organised' Church are insep-
arable.

The early Christian Creeds, I believe, have this clear implication. The faith of the Church expressed in these Creeds explicitly ascribes the Church to the work of the Holy Spirit. Indeed, several great theologians hold that the third part of the Creed affirms inseparably our faith in the Holy Spirit and our faith in the Holy Catholic Church, and that the sentence runs on without separation as follows: 'I believe in the Holy Spirit **in** the Holy Catholic Church . . .'

I am convinced that it is within the Church that I have received and have learned and come to love the Word of God in Scripture; just as it is within the Church that I have experienced the Church as communion, as community, as 'people made one in the unity of the Father, Son and the Holy Spirit', as St Cyprian puts it.

I must admit, however, that these experiences are not as widely shared within the Roman Catholic community as they should be. Despite the great efforts at all-round renewal of Christian life, particularly since the Vatican Council, there are still very many who do not regularly read and pray the Bible; many whose relationship with the Lord Jesus Christ is formal, rather than deeply personal; many whose experience of the Holy Spirit in their lives is distant and theoretical rather than warm and intimate; many who experience the Church too much as 'institution', and too little as community of love and grace and sharing of the gifts of the Spirit. Sadly, there are many who are hesitant about direct evangelisation, neglecting the Christian call to proclaim the Lord Jesus Christ openly and to spread the Good News of the Kingdom of God, as though they were 'ashamed of the gospel of Jesus Christ' and wanted to hide the light 'under a bushel'. The Evangelical Catholic Initiative, and the Evangelical movement in general, can contribute greatly to the life of the Church in all these respects.

Furthermore, and in spite of all the pleas and efforts of the leaders of the Churches, there are many in all the Churches whose attitudes to unity between Christians are more of apathy than enthusiasm, more of indifference than of commitment. The Evangelical Catholic Initiative, with the priority which it gives to fellowship with other Evangelicals, gives powerful witness and inspiration in this regard. It should be remembered, however, that the unity sought by the worldwide ecumenical movement is unity between Churches and not just between like-minded individuals within Churches and independently of Churches. The latter carries with it the risk of leading to still further fragmentation within Churches rather than to growth in unity between them. Real inter-Church fellowship and unity must be based on speaking and living the truth in love; and, though we must respect the truth as cherished by others, we must not fear to speak and live our own truth, so long as we do it in love. Ecumenical charity must respect the seriously-held convictions and the regulations and disciplines and, when necessary, self-denials, which spring from those convictions, in our respective Churches. This too is what the Holy Spirit is saying to the Churches, above all as we approach the great Jubilee of our Redemption in the year 2000.

A great Christian writer, philosopher and scientist of our time, Teilhard de Chardin, said, speaking of unity between Christians: 'Whatever rises must converge'. As we, in all the Churches, lift up our eyes and our hearts to the same Lord and Saviour on the Cross, we, in and with our Churches, must converge in Him; for He has said:

> 'When I am lifted up from the earth
> I shall draw all to myself.'
> (John 12:32)

FOREWORD

REV KEN NEWELL

*Minister of Fitzroy Presbyterian Church,
University Street, Belfast*

The book you are holding is a miracle. I've lived in Ireland for fifty-five years and can't ever recall coming across anything quite like it. I have seen some books of essays written by theologians from different Churches, but never have I opened a volume of Catholic testimonies commended with such warmth and respect by Protestants.

Given the horrific events of the last thirty years, when political and religious divisions have deepened and communities have been traumatised and hardened, miracle is a fair description.

The real miracle, however, is not just the contents of the book but the network of strong relationships that lie behind it. I feel greatly honoured to write this Foreword because many of the contributors are my personal friends. We have worked together for years on projects of an evangelical, charismatic and ecumenical nature. We know each other well.

But the miracle is deeper than friendship. We have discovered each other as brothers and sisters in Christ. We feel that we belong to each other; our heavenly Father has only one family and we are all part of it; Jesus Christ has only one body and we are all members of it; the Holy Spirit has only one temple and we are all stones in its structure.

The bonding to which this book bears witness is neither sentimental nor pietistic. The writers are people of courage and vision. By their lives and ministries they are challenging the harsh realities of Ireland's ancient animosities. Their names are well known for being at the forefront of reconciliation initiatives in Ireland. They are at the cutting edge of Christian witness, taking risks for peace, attempting to influence those prone to violence and encouraging them to pursue a more democratic approach.

Within their own faith-communities they are confronting the sectarian mind-set that still dominates; they are urging the abolition of the abusive theological language found in historic Church Articles and Confessions of Faith; they are pressing Christians to involve themselves more convincingly in the peacemaking vocation which is the mark of God's children (Matthew 5:9).

One of the challenges that this book will present to you is whether you are willing to allow Christ to make you an instrument of His peace and healing in a country that is still deeply distressed and wounded.

May the Christ whose first miracle was to turn water into wine in Cana of Galilee, turn us into agents of His peace, expressions of His love and ministers of His joy. That will be Ireland's greatest miracle.

COMMENDATIONS

BISHOP HAROLD MILLER

Church of Ireland Bishop of Down and Dromore

I am writing this 'testimony' almost exactly a year after that fateful day, 18th February, 1997, when I was elected Bishop of Down and Dromore. The election came as a great surprise, not only to me, but also to many of my friends and there are even one or two stories of people almost crashing their cars with the shock as they heard the announcement on Radio Ulster. The shock, I imagine, was because the adjectives I would most naturally use to describe the form of Christianity which 'clicks' in my own life would be 'evangelical' and 'charismatic' and perhaps it is not expected that too many bishops will be found in that particular school of thinking! However, that is simply how it is in my own life and the story I tell will perhaps show why.

An elder child of two rather-more-elderly-than-usual parents, I was brought up on the Shore Road in Belfast. My birth was in 1950, along with a new generation of baby-boomers after the war. We were the generation who had never had it so good and expected things to go on improving *ad infinitum*. Nevertheless, the world into which I was born was a simple world. My own family never owned a car, a fridge, a washing machine or any other modern devices, apart from a black-and-white television which arrived in 1959, within the first weeks of Ulster Television broadcasting. Our simple pleasures were going to school, playing in the street, Saturday afternoon westerns at the Lido cinema and the social life offered by the church.

Like many Ulster families, we were denominational mongrels. My mother was the offspring of a Catholic

father and a Congregationalist mother. However, her
father was killed in a train crash in Chicago when she
was only five (he had gone to set up a new life for them
in America) and she was brought up in Sandy Row,
Belfast in St Aidan's Church of Ireland. That had rather
turned her against evangelicalism, which reminded her
of a particular rector who taught her to sing:

> We don't drink, or smoke, or chew,
> Because we love our Lord!

Since she regularly committed at least the middle of the
three sins, that was that! My father, on the other hand,
was a Methodist, as all the Millers were, through and
through. Mind you, he too had been turned against anything evangelical and would have partly blamed the
preaching of the famous W. P. Nicholson. I think my
own embracing of the evangelical way must have been
difficult for both of them and indeed may well have been
part of my own teenage rebellion.

It happened when I was fifteen, through an organisation in the local Greencastle Methodist Church, called
The Boys Brigade. I loved the BB and was in it from the
age of seven. My friends were there, we played games,
did PE, drill, went on camps and learnt skills for life. It
was teriffic. In July 1965, we were on a camp in Port Erin,
Isle of Man and on the last morning of that camp, after
the prayers, we were invited to make a decision to give
our lives to Jesus Christ. I don't remember what the subject of the teaching was that morning. I only remember
being sure that it was the right thing to do. If Jesus Christ
loved me enough to die for me, then the least I could do
was give my life for Him. There have been many big
days in my life since – marriage, the birth of my children,
ordination, birthdays and so forth; but for me, I think
24th July 1965 will always remain the most important –
the day when I came to a living faith in a living Lord. As
the song goes:

> *O happy day, that fixed my choice*
> *On thee, my Saviour and my God!*

But that, thirty-three years ago, was only the beginning. Eventually, I moved from Belfast to study English and Philosophy at Trinity College, Dublin. Those were great years. Those were the years of 'broadening out', of meeting people from a whole range of backgrounds (I had flatmates from England and Mauritius), political and religious affiliations. They were also the post-Vatican II years, with the results of the Council gradually filtering into Ireland. I clearly remember the move from the personal reading of the Bible being discouraged by the Catholic Church, to the sales of what was then called (in the worst sexist language) *Good News for Modern Man*, with the Imprimatur, in paperback in bookshops in Dublin. And on top of all of that came Charismatic Renewal, which blew open so many of our presuppositions and denominational barriers. I can still see Liz, who was later to become my wife, rushing up to tell me about a meeting she had been at in Mount Street, full of Catholics praying in extempore prayer, just like the Brethren!

That was a wonderful time. In the late sixties and early seventies, nothing seemed impossible. We learned to speak in tongues, to open our lives to the renewing power of the Holy Spirit, to raise our hands in worship and to expect the Lord to speak in powerful ways into our lives in the here and now. We Protestants discovered that God was no respecter of persons and even poured out the Spirit on Roman Catholics! That was hard, because we thought they had got their theology wrong and no doubt it was hard the other way round too. But, once embraced, it was liberating. I even remember being pretty sure that the prayer of Jesus for the unity of the Church would be achieved in our day, as we together loved the One Lord and were baptized in the One Spirit. Sadly, somehow, it wasn't followed through, but I do wonder if, in our day, the word of God on this subject may yet come to us like Jonah *'for a second time'*.

So, to jump forward through many years in which God in His mercy had continued to have His hand on my life, through ordination, marriage, the birth of Kevin, Ciara, Laura and Niall, the death of my parents, ministry in Carrickfergus, Nottingham, Belfast and Cork; fortieth birthdays, twentieth anniversaries of ordination and marriage and the realisation that I am probably more than halfway through my active ministry, I come to February 1998. Here I am, a bishop in the Church of Ireland, in a situation in Ireland which desperately needs His reconciling love, in a situation in Western Europe which has been enveloped by secularism and yet in which people are on a desperate search for spirituality. And to that, I can only bring my own experience of the Lord, as a charismatic and evangelical Christian. I know what He has done in my life in the past. But, more than that, I know that He is the Christ who is with me, the same yesterday, today and forever; that He has so much more to teach me and I have so much more of Him to experience. In the Church of Ireland confirmation service, which I so often conduct now, the Confirmation Prayer seems to sum it up, when it asks God that we may

> *Daily increase in your Holy Spirit **more and more**
> Until we come to your everlasting Kingdom. Amen*

It is a thrill and joy for me to read in this book the stories of so many within the Roman Catholic tradition whose experience is similar to my own. These are people who have discovered, as I have discovered, the evangelical truth, that we are brought into a right relationship with a heavenly Father, not by anything we do, but by a simple and liberating trust in our common Saviour.

Of course there are still doctrinal differences to be thought through; there are still denominational affiliations in our backgrounds and ecclesiastical structures

which can keep us apart. But, at the end of the day, the
same Jesus, who broke down all barriers, not least the
dividing wall of partition between Jews and Gentiles,
has already brought into a united family all His
redeemed children; and our 'Catholic' and 'Protestant'
distinctives are as nothing in God's sight in comparison
to the oneness of all believers. At the foot of the Cross,
orange and green, Republican and Unionist, Catholic
and Protestant meet as sinners who need and come to
know what it is to be saved by grace.

Rev Dr Trevor W. J. Morrow

Presbyterian minister, Lucan, Co. Dublin

Lambeg, near Belfast where I was reared, was almost one hundred per cent Protestant. I went to Protestant schools, I played Protestant sports like rugby and cricket. As a family we voted as Protestants, for a Protestant parliament, for a Protestant people. I attended a Protestant (Presbyterian) church. There may have been Roman Catholics in Lambeg but I certainly didn't know any. There was nothing unusual about my upbringing in Northern Ireland in the 1950s and 1960s.

It was in this context, in a good Christian home and while attending a sound Presbyterian church, that I responded as a child to the invitation to know Jesus as my personal Saviour and Lord. In those days, there were two things about which I was convinced. The first was that being a Protestant didn't make one a Christian and the second was that being a Roman Catholic meant you definitely were not. A real Christian was someone who had been 'born again' and had responded to the gospel by receiving Jesus as Saviour and Lord. When I say that we were convinced that Roman Catholics were not Christians, it was not based on personal experience. I didn't know any Roman Catholics, but we knew about them. They were not to be trusted – for their loyalty was to another country, the Irish Republic. They were liable to be unemployed; either because they were lazy or because, due to their having such large families, it was in their interests, because of the social benefits, not to work. They were not as clean and tidy as us – hence the common expression, 'wash your face, clean yourself up and make yourself a bit more Protestant looking!' But, most of all, they had a religion which was as deviant and heterodox as any weird sect, like the Mormons or the Jehovah's Witnesses. This was all reinforced by fiery preachers who would unveil Jesuit conspiracies and immorality behind convent walls and would introduce to us 'converted Roman Catholics' who would give thrilling testimonies under the slogan 'from Rome to Christ'. All this underlined our prejudices and suspicions about 'the other sort'.

Lucan, near Dublin, where I now live and minister, is predominantly Roman Catholic. Fifteen years ago, I left Northern Ireland and came to what the prophet Jonah would have called his Nineveh. God had called me to work among people who, in terms of my past, were culturally, politically and religiously alienated from me. They were different. The truth was, I had no idea how to begin this ministry. What is a reformed Church meant to do – try and make everyone Presbyterian? How was I to relate to a culture and sub-culture of which I was totally ignorant?

God's answer to my need was outrageous and, on His part, quite mischievous. During my second week in Lucan, I had cause to visit a school in the next village. The school was Colaiste Ciaran in Leixlip. We had a few children from my church in attendance there. When I entered the staff room, I was warmly greeted by the Roman Catholic chaplain. He sat me down and within a few minutes he began to tell me his story. It was, in the language of my upbringing, a testimony to the saving grace of God. He related how, on one Good Friday, he had cried out to God for mercy and had invited Jesus Christ to be the Lord of his life. The result had been a radical change in perspective and behaviour.

I had heard many testimonies like this before but not from a Roman Catholic priest. However I responded, it was obviously with excitement and delight. In fact, Fr. Dermot O'Gorman (that was his name) came to my house a few days later and asked if we could meet together since we obviously shared something that he had difficulty sharing with some of his fellow priests. So Dermot and I began to meet every Monday at 4.00 p.m. in my home. We read and studied the Scriptures, we prayed for and encouraged each other. I had discovered not only a priest who was my brother in Christ, but that God, in His amazing providence, had so arranged our lives that a member of a Sacred Order from Kilkenny should become a 'Barnabas' to a Presbyterian from Lambeg. This was so that I might be better equipped to minister in a Roman Catholic context.

My encounter with Fr. Dermot O'Gorman has been repeated on numerous occasions with various clergy and lay folk from the Catholic community. Similarly the testimonies in this book have the hallmarks of the authentic work of grace.

For Presbyterians like myself, who still hold to the principle of the Reformation – of justification by faith alone, the implications are straightforward. If these testimonies are evidence of real faith in Christ, then whatever our theological differences, these Roman Catholic believers are justified by faith alone, and so are our brothers and sisters in Christ.

In Paul's letter to the Galatians, he saw this doctrine as vital for Christian fellowship and freedom. The Jewish Christians from Jerusalem had come down to Galatia and were fearful that Paul's message of justification apart from the work of the law would undermine the traditions and identity of their Jewish inheritance. They were insisting that it was not enough for a Gentile to believe in Jesus Christ. They also had to follow the laws of Judaism; to be circumcised, to keep the dietary requirements, to observe the Jewish sabbaths and festivals, in order for them to be accepted as Christians. It became for them a criteria for fellowship. Paul rails against this. If someone insists that something else is required, apart from faith, in order to accept a person as a fellow Christian, or as a basis for fellowship, then they, says Paul, are preaching a false gospel.

The social and peer pressure on many Presbyterians, particularly in Northern Ireland, is akin to that experienced by the apostle Peter in Antioch, as Paul records it in his letter to the Galatians. Peter knew and believed the gospel of grace, but for fear of what others would think of him, he withdrew from fellowship with the Gentile believers, because they did not conform to the practices of Judaism. Paul is so outraged by this that he confronts Peter face to face on this issue.

Many evangelicals within the reformed Churches would not deny the reality of the faith of these genuine Catholic people, but are hesitant to embrace them as fellow believers in Christ for fear of what other Protestants would say or think. Some have gone further and have rewritten the gospel by suggesting that faith alone is not enough for Roman Catholics. They must be able to articulate clearly the reformation doctrine of justification and be willing to leave the Catholic Church before they can be accepted as fellow members of the body of Christ. This, according to Paul, is a different gospel.

It is therefore, on the material principle of the Reformation, that a person is justified by faith alone, and for the sake of the gospel, that I, as a Presbyterian, unequivocally accept and affirm with joy and enthusiasm these Roman Catholic believers as my brothers and sisters in Christ.

Pastor Paul Reid

Paul Reid is the leader of the Lifelink team, a group of churches in Ireland committed to church planting and resourcing other churches. He is also Senior Pastor of Christian Fellowship Church in Belfast.

I am grateful that my parents, although not Christians, ensured that my sister and I went to Sunday School. Both sets of grandparents belonged to the Open Brethren and this was the predominant influence on my younger days. The Brethren always maintained a strict policy of separation from most things: the world, other professing Christians and anything that looked vaguely suspicious! On being asked one day did we have problems with Roman Catholics, I replied that we had problems with Baptists!

I was brought up to believe that I had a deep need in my life that could only be filled by a personal relationship with Christ. I attended frequent 'gospel missions' where the emphasis was on being born again (John 3) and getting saved. The Brethren have an Anabaptist belief which has no place for children being included in the community of faith until they have a personal conversion experience. This can occur at any age, even three or four, but they would not normally be received into church membership, or be baptised by total immersion, until their teens.

After a period of rebellion, against religion in general, during my early to middle teens, I was saved at the age of sixteen on the 27th October 1967. I had largely stopped going to church, when a great-uncle phoned to ask if I would go to a special series of gospel meetings in Drumaness, outside Ballynahinch, Co. Down. For some reason I said yes and after the first evening was challenged about the emptiness in my life. I had started a regular round of getting drunk every weekend with my friends, but when I sobered up I always felt God 'speaking' to me about the Cross. The fact that God loved me so much that He sent His Son to die for me always had an impact on me. I knew I needed to respond in a personal way and not just give a mental assent.

One day at school, during a class discussion, I found myself preaching to my whole class about the need of a personal Saviour. Someone asked me if I was a Christian, as defined by myself, and I said no. They all laughed at me. It is possible to know all about Christianity but not have a personal relationship with the Lord Jesus. Thirty years ago I made that commitment and it changed my life. Knowing my sins forgiven, being saved, changed my attitudes and it soon became noticeable. At school I was called Billy Graham because of my evangelistic zeal. I had found Christ and I wanted others to know Him too.

An aunt invited me to a Sunday Bible Class consisting of teenagers my own age. Three days after my conversion, at this Bible Class, I met Priscilla (age fourteen) who was to become my wife seven years later! We got on with what young Christian people did in our circles, going to meetings, teaching Sunday School, running meetings for children and teenagers, giving our testimonies at gospel meetings, all with a view to seeing others converted.

It was when Priscilla went to Queen's University, Belfast that I first met other Christians from the mainline denominations on a regular basis. The Brethren accepted that there were Christians in every denomination (except the Roman Catholic Church perhaps) but that on church practice, government etc they were wrong. A dreadful spirit of 'we are right and everybody else is wrong', clouded our thinking. Ours was the only visible local church which the Lord recognised as a valid New Testament Church, although we believed in the Universal Church to which every true believer in Christ belonged. My father-in-law, although Brethren himself, taught me to accept Christians from every tradition. It was a hard lesson to learn. I remember being asked to speak at a Youth Service in a Presbyterian church, I refused on the grounds that I didn't agree with some of their practices!

We left the Brethren in 1981 to form a House Church in Carryduff where we lived. The Lord had been working in our lives and we were looking for something more. We didn't expect what was to follow. I was baptised in the Holy Spirit at a conference called Spring Harvest in 1983. I had come from a place of actively opposing this experience in the Brethren. We took a strictly 'cessation position', i.e. all the miraculous signs, gifts in the Bible, e.g. tongues, prophesy, healing ceased at the end of the first century. New vistas opened up for me. This was the doorway to a new dynamic realm of spiritual life. This was as radical as my conversion sixteen years before.

When you begin to move in charismatic circles and go to certain meetings you meet people from every background. It was here that I began to meet Catholics. I discovered that many of them loved and served Jesus the way I did. I was confused. My first experience of a charismatic-type meeting had been back in the early seventies. We saw an advertisement in the *Belfast Telegraph* about a Christian musical called *Come Together*, featuring Pat Boone. We didn't realise at the time what this was about, although we knew Pat Boone was a Christian. When we got there people were waving their hands in the air, singing in a strange language and, worst of all, there were nuns! Afraid a nun might hug me, we left after about fifteen minutes. Anything with nuns at it couldn't be right.

Rev Cecil Kerr has had a profound effect on changing attitudes in Ireland. His work at the Renewal Centre, along with his wife Myrtle, has been for many years a light on sectarian bigotry within the Church. Cecil came to CFC to speak and helped me greatly. He, along with Rev Ken Newell introduced me to different groups of Catholic believers and I began to see them for what they were.

On one occasion I had been asked to chair a meeting of 'Evangelicals and Catholics in Dialogue', an annual event run by Ken Newell and others. It was uncharted waters for me and I was a little nervous. Ken introduced me to one of the speakers, Rev Padraig McCarthy, a priest with ECI and based in Rathdrum, Co. Wicklow, and then suggested I take him out to meet the reception committee at the door! 'It's a joke,' I thought, but alas it wasn't. A group of protesters had gathered at the entrance. They were not exactly hostile, but distinctly unfriendly. We were greeted politely, but with a barrage of questions. 'What about the Mass, Mary, confession, purgatory?' The list seemed endless. But the focus soon fixed on the question – Can you be a 'real' Christian and a member of the Catholic Church at the same time? 'Absolutely not,' our protagonists cried in unison.

Padraig wondered aloud who were the real Christians. He said he believed that salvation was through faith in Christ alone PLUS nothing and no one. However, he observed that the protesters believed that salvation was found in Christ plus NOT belonging to the Catholic Church, which was tantamount to a doctrine of salvation through works! An eerie silence ensued until one of the protesters, a clergyman, finally conceded the point and was at once set upon by his colleagues. Padraig and I beat a quiet retreat back into the meeting.

Something was beginning to dawn on me. When a person confesses Jesus Christ as Lord, they are received with a wild extravagant love. Angels rejoice in Heaven. The Father, in welcoming the prodigal, provides new clothes, shoes, a ring and a party! That's the way we were accepted and we are commanded to show the same acceptance to those who love the same Master. We may not always use the same terminology but we share a common experience of Christ. It is time to acknowledge such as our brothers and sisters in Christ. 'Accept one another . . . just as Christ accepted you, in order to bring praise to God' (Romans 15:7). If Christ has forgiven and accepted a person, then I accept them too – not grudgingly acknowledge they may know Christ. I was beginning to know what Jesus was talking about in John 17:20. 'I pray also for those who will believe in me . . . that all of them may be one, Father, just as you are in me and I am in you.'

Dr John Kyle, recently returned (1993) from London, introduced me to Larry Kelly of the Lamb of God Community in Belfast. Here I found a home where we worshipped, prayed and talked together. I then met a priest, Paul Symonds (see Paul Symond's testimony on page 222), and when, together, we officiated at a wedding something finally struck me. Here was someone who not only followed and served the same Lord as I did but I could see by his life and testimony that he knew Jesus in a way I didn't! I had to humble myself and acknowledge my own self-righteousness. God is at work in every church. None of us has a monopoly on Him and my only regret is that I didn't see it years ago.

There are, of course, genuinely held differences and it doesn't help unity to pretend they don't exist. However I believe that those of us in the 'New Churches' need not only to acknowledge and respect what is happening in the Catholic Church but to do our part to encourage a fresh spiritual awakening. We can do this by concentrating our evangelistic efforts in Ireland on the increasing number of people who have no Christian profession or church commitment. We need to, as far as we can, work together in seeing the Kingdom of God built in a new way. God has His servants in every Church, we must speak well of each other, acknowledge what God has done in each others' lives and stand together.

I commend this book to all. Paddy Monaghan and the members of the Evangelical Catholic Initiative are to be encouraged in all they are seeking to do. The testimonies contained in these pages are thrilling and exciting. I know many of the contributors personally and have seen firsthand what Jesus has done in and through their lives. We have something in common, or rather someone in common, Jesus Christ, as Lord and Saviour. I am proud to own them as brothers and sisters in Christ. Their testimonies will bring glory to God and if others, from whatever background, were to emulate their commitment to Christ, Ireland would truly be changed.

REV DR KEN WILSON

Superintendent of Dun Laoghaire
Methodist Church District

My own faith journey began, I suppose, before I was born! My parents dedicated me to God in baptism and promised to give me 'access to the worship and teaching of the church', that I might, in the words of the old Baptismal Service, *'come to the knowledge of Christ my Saviour and enter into the full fellowship of them that believe'.* So my parents provided a Christian home and the Methodist Church provided the teaching of the Bible on the love of God for every person. It was impressed upon me that I needed to respond in a personal way to all that Jesus had done through his Cross and empty tomb. As I look back, it seems almost inevitable that I indeed accepted God's free gift of salvation as a child of fourteen, when I was being prepared for full membership of the Church. As Ephesians 2 says: *'Because of his great love for us, God, who is rich in mercy, made us alive with Christ even when we were dead in transgressions – it is by grace you have been saved.'* St Paul repeats this: *'For it is by grace you have been saved – and this is not from yourselves, it is the gift of God – not by works, so that no-one can boast'* (Ephesians 2:4, 5, 8, 9).

Later, in my teens, I was encouraged to make a fuller commitment to Jesus, largely through an interdenominational mission group – The Faith Mission. The emphasis at this time was on holiness and the work of the Holy Spirit. Many hours were spent each week in prayer and meditation on the Bible, both on my own and at prayer meetings. These meetings, together with the opportunity to preach most Sundays, convinced me of a call from

God to missionary work. After training at Edgehill Theological College in Belfast, the Methodist Seminary, I spent eleven years doing pastoral and evangelistic work in the West Indies. I returned to Ireland in 1977 and have served as a Methodist minister in Cullybackey, Glenburn (Belfast), Lisburn and Bray, Co. Wicklow. My highest calling is to offer Christ to all types of men and women in the hope that they will crown Him King and Lord of their lives.

It took me many years to discover that there is only one Church of Jesus Christ to which all who trust in Jesus belong. Often, with tongue in cheek, I traced my reluctant journey in this way: at fourteen years, when I made a child-like commitment to Jesus, one of the things I believed about God was that He was **not a Roman Catholic!** Later, when I was influenced by Christians from other Protestant Churches I came to see that God **was not a Methodist!** In the West Indies I discovered that He was **not a white middle-class Englishman!** Later still, I learned that he was **not even a Protestant!** We cannot put God in a box and behave as though our side 'owned' Him.

I have been asked for a personal response to the messages of personal testimony in this publication. Truth to tell, I was moved to tears as I read them. Here are stories of enormous power and energy. Here we read of the chains of sin and destructive habits being broken; of broken bodies being healed; of the Holy Spirit's power being manifest in very 'ordinary' people; of prejudice and hatred being overcome. We read of the victory of Christian love in the hearts of those who have been devastated by the violence in our land. As an evangelical Christian, I warm to the accounts of deep personal faith in Jesus Christ. I see here clear witness to the all-sufficiency of our Lord's death and resurrection when it comes to our deepest need: that is, how can sin be forgiven and how can we know peace with God? Here, in language which anyone can understand, are accounts of men and women who put their trust, not in the external religious rituals of Christianity, but in Jesus Christ as personal Lord and Saviour.

It is for others with greater knowledge to speak of how widespread this 'evangelical awakening' in the Catholic Church has become. There are many serious differences between the Catholic and Protestant Churches and we accept this fact openly and honestly. However, when one meets Christ in the heart of one's 'enemy', then he or she cannot be an enemy any longer! At that point of personal encounter, one realises with joy that one has met a brother or sister in Christ.

In my humble opinion, such an awakening, which is so closely tied in with a thirst for Bible knowledge, can only be greeted with warmth and enthusiasm among Protestant evangelicals. As a Methodist I unreservedly commend this publication to all those with concerns about the Protestant–Catholic divide. Here is the language of the 'warmed heart' which would be at home in any of our testimony meetings.

1

BURY YOUR PRIDE WITH MY SON

MICHAEL MCGOLDRICK

*Father of Michael McGoldrick (Junior), who, freshly
graduated from Queen's University, who had been working,
while studying, as a part-time taxi driver to support
his child and his wife, then pregnant with their second child.
He was shot dead in a random killing by Loyalist
paramilitaries on July 8th, 1996, in the aftermath
of the 'Drumcree Standoff''.*

Bridie and I went to Warrenpoint on our annual holiday
– we have a caravan there and have taken our holidays
there for many years. We were enjoying our holiday
when, on Monday July 8th, 1996, I turned on the television and read on the teletext news: 'Lurgan taxi driver
murdered.' Bridie and I just stared at each other, our
hearts in turmoil. Our son Michael had taken a job as a
part-time taxi driver in Lurgan, while studying for his
degree at university. Bridie said: 'If it had been anyone
belonging to us, we would surely have known by now.'
We remained glued to the TV and radio and waited anx-
iously for any further developments.

Later on in the morning came the news we were
dreading. The news bulletin on the radio gave more
information: '. . . early thirties, married with one child . . .
wife expecting another . . . just graduated from Queen's
University . . .' It was our son, our only child. We were
so shocked that we just started screaming and shouting.
I ran out of the caravan. I remember going down on my
knees and hitting the ground with my fists. I looked up

to Heaven and shouted at God: 'Hanging on the cross was nothing compared to what I am going through!' I was so angry and in such shock that I actually mocked the Lord. I thought that our pain was the greatest pain that anyone could ever bear. I said to Bridie in a moment of despair, 'We'll never laugh or smile again.'

It's very hard to describe how I felt at this time – burdened and low. I loved my son so much, and now he had been taken away from us. The thought that we would not see him again was too much to bear. It was the saddest time of my life. At the wake, and before they put the lid on the coffin I went up to the coffin and, putting my two hands on top of his, I said: 'Goodbye, son, I'll see you in Heaven.' As I said this, it was as if a great power went through me – I haven't a clue what it was – it wasn't earthly, that's for sure. It was as if I had been filled with a great sense of joy and confidence in God. I felt as if I could have faced Goliath – I never felt as strong in my whole life. If anybody had said, 'Michael, you're not able to carry your son's coffin', I would have said, 'Nothing in this world is going to stop me from carrying my son's coffin'.

After the funeral, I saw a film crew filming. There was a lot of activity because of the Drumcree standoff. I knew I had to go over to them. I had a message to give. That morning I had written on an envelope a word which came so calmly and clearly to me: 'Bury your pride with my son.' At the bottom I wrote: 'Forgive them.' I felt that, despite the agony we were going through, God had given me a message of peace, forgiveness and reconciliation.

I didn't want the people who had murdered Michael to devastate another family. Bridie and I received the grace and power to forgive Michael's killers publicly. I knew it was the Holy Spirit speaking to us through the words of Jesus: 'Forgive them, for they know not what they do.' The words from the Our Father also kept ringing in my ear: 'Forgive us our trespasses as we forgive those who trespass against us.'

Nothing is worse than seeing your own child going into the ground. I said to the TV reporters that I forgave whoever had taken Michael's life, and I still forgive them. I now know that, at that time, an awful lot of people around the world were praying for me. I experienced a power and a grace to forgive from my heart, and it was such a freedom and release. I know that resentment and bitterness would have killed me.

The day of the funeral, July 11th, was the worst day of my life. I felt so low, despondent and depressed. The following day, as was my custom, I took my dog for a walk. As I walked, I found this deep laughter welling up inside me. It was like a deep inexpressible joy, which came from within. As this joy and laughter took hold, I said to myself: 'Why am I laughing? I should be the last person in the world to be laughing.' I know people will think this was just going over the top – some kind of trauma brought on by grief. But it wasn't. It was as if my son was laughing in me, and I was giving expression to it. That's the only way I could describe what was happening to me. I know if anybody told me this story, I too would find it hard to believe, because I am a logical, pragmatic kind of person. I too wanted a reason to make sense of my experience – there is no logical reason why one day I should be the unhappiest man in the whole of Ireland, and the next day feel so happy and joyful. On the way home, I felt so good it was as if I was walking on air. I thought to myself, 'If I'm going to die, I want it to be now!' I felt as if I had received an abundance of God's grace and the joy of the Holy Spirit. People must have thought that I was going mad!

What is strange is that, a few hours later, I went out again for a walk and almost the complete opposite came over me – a deep despair. It was horrible. I put my head in my hands and thought, 'What's wrong with me? Why am I feeling this way?' It was as if I was being shown two sides of life – one of light, the other of darkness. The only prayer I could think of was the 'act of contrition'. I prayed: 'O my God, I am heartily sorry for having offended Thee. I detest my sins above every other evil, because they displease Thee, O my God, who, for Thine infinite goodness are so deserving of all my love. I firmly resolve never more to offend Thee and to amend my life.'

When I prayed the act of contrition, I felt as if something was leaving me – it reminded me of a snake shedding its outer skin! I was so exhausted after this experience that I had to go to bed. The following day, I realised that just as I had offered forgiveness to those who killed my son, so I knew that God had forgiven me my sin. After this experience, the joy I had known returned (not as intense as before) and all I wanted to do was to be alone and pray and read my Bible.

I had, and still have, a clear grasp of the horror of sin, and I remember saying to God: 'These hands will never do any evil again.' I got a clean slate that night – I could not even think of sinning. I had no desire to. People talk about conversions. I now know what a conversion is. Before Michael's death, I had not been very interested in my faith. But, since his death, I go to Mass almost every day.

Some weeks after all these events, I went to a prayer meeting to witness to what had happened in my life. I met a man who takes clothing and food from here to the Ukraine and Romania. I was so struck by what he shared about his work of reaching out and caring for the poor that I said to him, 'I have to go there as well to help.' I have since gone out on a number of trips distributing aid and have been working as a volunteer at home, gathering material. I place appeals for foodstuffs, clothing, toys etc. in parish bulletins in the nearby towns of Portadown, Lurgan and Craigavon. I then pick up whatever is handed in at various designated collection points and transport it to a large warehouse in an industrial estate in Craigavon, Co. Armagh, which we are allowed to use, rent-free. When we have gathered and sorted enough for a full fifteen-ton lorry load, and when the necessary £2,500 for transport costs has been scraped together, we dispatch the load to the Ukraine, to Romania or Bulgaria. To date, sixteen lorry loads of aid have been distributed. The work is cross-denominational, both Protestant and Catholic people being very much involved in the donating, collecting, sorting and transporting of the goods. Lasting friendships, across denominational barriers, have been built up in the process. People have been pulled together in their desire to respond to the desperate need of others. On arrival at its destination, the aid is distributed through Baptist, Pentecostal and Roman Catholic channels to those in greatest need.

Since Michael's death, I have been a changed man. I feel as if I have been taken hold of by Christ, and I now want to take hold of Christ and give my life to loving God and serving His people.

2

THIS SICKNESS IS NOT UNTO DEATH

SR. ANNA MARY HANNON

*Sr. Anna Mary, former Portadown based
Provincial of the Franciscan Sisters, is currently
Co-ordinator of Assisi House, a Franciscan
retirement home in Dublin.*

'The word of God is alive and active. It cuts more finely than any double-edged sword; it penetrates even to dividing soul and spirit, joints and marrow; it judges the thoughts and attitudes of the heart' (Hebrews 4:12).

I was born in a little thatched house on a small farm in the middle of a bog in County Galway in 1939. I was the youngest of four children. My mother was a very religious type of woman and told me stories of the saints when I was a child. The Lord's hand was in all of this because these stories were part of the foundation that was laid for my future walk in life. My mother died when I was ten years old and that affected me deeply. Her dying words to me were, 'Anna Mary, always remember the "golden rule".' I knew well what that meant, since it was very much the rule of our household: *'Never do to anyone what you would not want done to yourself.'* My father fulfilled the role of father and mother to me and instilled in me the need to speak lovingly of people, or not to speak at all. My only recollection of his scolding me was when I once spoke negatively about the girl next door.

God and the things of God were very much part of
our daily life and conversation in my humble home. If
we complained about the weather or some such thing,
we were told we should be saying, 'Thanks be to God'.
This seemed to be the answer to everything. My father
would not have known that wonderful line in Scripture
where it tells us that 'we enter His gates with thanksgiving in our hearts . . .' and yet he lived it!

Shortly after my mother died, I was asked by a local
group to dance during the interval of a play they were
staging in our local hall. After much pressure, I very
reluctantly agreed. Before my turn came, another girl got
up to dance and there was great applause. My thoughts
then were, 'When I get up and dance a little, they will
applaud me too . . . What would happen if I were to give
my whole self to God for others?' In a flash, I was
brought back to the story of St Francis going down the
streets of Assisi, singing his heart out in love for his God
and drawing many people to God. I decided that night in
my heart that I would be a Franciscan Sister. I hadn't a
clue what that entailed, but I knew in my heart that I
would only be happy if I followed the call I felt I received
that night.

When I left school, I followed that call and tried to be
faithful to all that was required of me. A lot of my training involved the study of Scripture and theology. I
worked hard and was awarded top grades. However, it
was all head knowledge. I did try very hard to be a 'good
religious' and was faithful in my prayer, meditation,
times of silence, etc. I was always striving to be virtuous
and, of course, never succeeding!

When a call came from our Superior for volunteers
for our mission in Egypt, I was very enthusiastic and
offered to go there. I was young and lively, loved the life
and thought I could bring great changes in that mission!
It was unenlightened zeal but, like that of Paul, the Lord
could use it. I wasn't long in Egypt when I discovered
that I couldn't change anyone, not even myself! That was

why I was open when a Jesuit priest came back from his
holidays in the United States on the Feast of Epiphany,
January 6th, 1971 and shared about the wave of the Spirit
that was moving across the United States and elsewhere.
He talked about the power of the Holy Spirit to change
our lives and the lives of others. It was just what I needed. We talked about it after the Eucharist and decided we
should meet to pray for this outpouring of the Spirit. As
a result, we decided to meet and study the Acts of the
Apostles and find out what they did. A Coptic Catholic
Sister, a Jesuit priest, a Presbyterian minister and his wife
and I began to meet every week to read the Scriptures
and pray.

Shortly after we began, a woman from Zambia came
to visit the American School where the Presbyterian minister and his wife worked. She very evidently had what
we wanted and so we invited her to our prayer meeting
to pray with and for us. She came with her ten-year-old
son and, at the end of the meeting, we asked her to pray
over us for the release of the Spirit, whom we knew to be
present in our lives, but who seemed to be somehow
locked up somewhere there! She did so and nothing
extraordinary happened for any of us at that time, but
we just believed that the Lord had heard that prayer and
were happy about it. However, as I read a passage of
Scripture to the Sisters after the meal that evening, the
words suddenly came alive for me. I shall never forget
the particular line that spoke as never before to me:
'Preserve me Lord, for I take refuge in you.' Though I
had studied Scripture for years and had read it every day
since becoming a Sister, this was the first time it had really come alive for me. This created a new hunger in me for
the Word of God and I read, studied and prayed the
Scriptures every spare moment I had. It was really exciting. A new joy sprang up inside me and what seemed
very difficult before suddenly didn't seem so difficult.
Everything in my own religious tradition took on a new
meaning for me.

Besides this, I got to know so many Christians of other denominations and came to value their traditions too. In Egypt there are many different Christain traditions, but we all met and prayed and got to know the Lord and one another in deeper and deeper ways as we continued to be faithful to our prayer meetings. We made lasting friendships and continue to keep in touch, even though most of us have now left Egypt. The Lord showed me early on in my walk with Him that we are all parts of the same Body, the Body of Christ and He is the Head. We are the members and all have our different roles to play in the building up of this Body. Just as in the human body the different members look different and function differently, so too it is with us. Nonetheless, we are all parts of that one Body. In the Lord, we are one. It is we who have done the dividing. We concentrate too much on our various functions, instead of looking to our Head and taking our orders from Him.

In my initial walk with the Lord, I depended greatly on authors who were not Roman Catholics. Watchman Nee was a great teacher, as was David DuPlessy, Smith Wigglesworth, Jessie Penn-Lewis, Merlin Carothers, Andrew Murray and many others. For me my experience in Egypt was very different to that of the Israelites. They were led out of Egypt to be freed from bondage, while I was led into Egypt to be freed from bondage! If I were to spend all my days and nights thanking God, it would not be enough to express the gratitude I feel in my heart for such a great gift.

I had to leave Egypt five years after this experience because of serious illness. There was actually no hope for my recovery and I have discovered since then that many of my Sisters in the Congregation were praying for a happy death for me at that time! When I was in hospital and feeling very ill, with doctors not knowing what to do and wishing I would die, I opened my New Testament one night, as usual, and read: 'This sickness is not unto death but for the glory of God.'

Later, when the doctor came to tell me that there was nothing they could do for me, but that I had better get my charismatic friends to pray for me, I responded by saying that I wasn't going to die! You can imagine the reaction! However, I quoted the Lord's word and said that I didn't know what was going to happen to me, but I would hold on to that word and see what God would do. I knew that God would be glorified no matter what happened, but I didn't know how. It was months later, when I was in a little oratory in our Convent chapel, that a line I had read in a book shortly before that came back to me: 'God cannot not love me.' Something happened in my spirit just then and I actually danced with joy right there in the oratory! I was reminded of David at that moment and didn't mind who came in. Actually, nobody did, so I could relish the moment with my God. That was the beginning of a healing for me. No doctor could get the glory, no medicine could be quoted as being the remedy, only an experience of the love of the Lord. I continue to rejoice in and experience more and more of that love each day of my life and am very grateful to my Father for His constant love and affection for me: to Jesus, my Beloved Saviour, Deliverer, Rescuer, Healer; and to His Holy Spirit who prays for me, speaks for me, is wise for me, is everything I need to be like Jesus.

For seven years, up to 1997, I was Provincial of the Franciscan Convent in Portadown, Co. Armagh. The convent is situated in a Loyalist area, beside the headquarters of the feared Loyalist Volunteer Force, who oppose the current Peace Process. Our convent has an important ministry of reconciliation, expressed through the setting up of a nursing home catering for elderly Catholic and Protestants residents. The staff consists of skilled people drawn from both communities. One of the great blessings in my life is my friendship with Protestant and Pentecostal Christians. I have been blessed on many occasions by the honesty and intimacy of their friendship with the Lord and their deep love for the Scriptures.

Our present leader, Pope John Paul II, is very emphatic about our need to humble ourselves and reach out in repentance to the many brothers and sisters whom we have wounded so deeply in the past. My heart was broken by the tragedy of the intransigence of both sides of the community over the standoff arising from the Orange March in Dumcree, an area of Portadown. As a result, I felt led by the Lord to set up a service of healing in the Town Hall in Portadown on the last Sunday of June 1997, to help heal the many wounds of this divided community. A capacity crowd of over 300 people, from both sides of the community, filled the hall. Two victims of the violence in the North shared their faith in Jesus – Bernadette, a Catholic Christian whose husband was shot dead by Loyalist paramilitaries ten years ago and Alan, whose wife and father-in-law were both killed in the Shankhill bombing some three years previously. Bernadette shared how the Lord had helped her to forgive and pick up the pieces again in her life. Alan shared how, while he was still in the process of forgiveness, the Lord had helped him not to forsake his cross-community work, in spite of his awful personal tragedy. This was deeply challenging to the people present. During the service of healing we had a live link-up, by telephone, with some two-thousand Catholic and Protestant Christians, gathered in an East Belfast church to pray for healing in the land. I had the privilege of leading prayer for a breakthrough in our community. Praise God, we saw a wonderful answer to these and many other prayers over the summer period, enjoying, as we did, relative peace.

I have since moved to a Fransiscan Community in Dublin and am continuing to pursue the ministry of reconciliation, which is so very much on the Lord's heart. It is also explicitly urged upon us by Pope John Paul II. My heart goes out to the many victims of the violence, like Bernadette and Alan, and Deirdre Enright, left with two small children, whose husband was very much involved in cross-community work when he was murdered.

Since June 1997 I have had a constant physical pain in
my body, from which neither medication nor prayer has
as yet brought any relief. It is true, as Romans 8:28 says,
that all things work together for good, for those who love
the Lord. Thus this pain has been a constant reminder to
me of the great pain in the heart of God the Father, when
He sees the divisions in the Body of His Son here in
Ireland. The spectre of Ireland being known across the
nations of the world as a country where Catholic murders Protestant, and vice versa, is a major scandal to the
Name of Jesus. But, praise God, I believe that His Holy
Spirit is moving to melt our hard hearts and bring both
Catholic and Protestant back again to the centrality of a
personal relationship with Jesus Christ. Ireland, by His
grace, shall become again a 'light to the nations'.

From time to time I write to the head of the RUC and
some of the political leaders, just to encourage them in
their work, to let them know I'm praying for them and to
share some relevant portion of Scripture with them. This
has been much appreciated. I believe it is urgent for all of
us to take prayer seriously, for we are in a kairos moment
in which our country can slip back into civil war or else
come into spiritual revival and renewal, with the outworking of a just and fair political settlement in
Northern Ireland. How we need to come, Catholic and
Protestant together, before our God with that cry of the
psalmist on our lips: 'Preserve me Lord, for I take refuge
in you.'

3

YOUTH WITH A MISSION

ROB CLARKE

Rob was involved in the probation service in New Zealand before he came to Ireland. He is the Director of Youth With A Mission, Ireland, an interdenominational lay missionary organisation, with forty-two full-time workers in Ireland, of which fifty per cent are Catholic. YWAM runs retreats and various courses for training youth leaders.

I was born in 1956 in Wellington, New Zealand. I grew up as the third eldest in a Catholic family of nine children. I remember my early years as years of great fun and adventure. From an early age I felt the occasional stirrings towards God. Sometimes during Lent, I'd make a special effort to get up and attend early morning Mass. I also remember making some effort to say my prayers in the evening, before climbing into bed. As I grew older, life became filled with many competing interests, hobbies and sporting activities, all demanding attention. I took up surfing, tramping and karate in my early teens, and also played rugby for my college. During these years, I experienced some disillusionment with my faith. Mass ceased to mean very much to me, and the attractions of girls, alcohol and sport started to dominate my life.

My older sisters got involved in the 'Young Christian Workers' movement, a faith-support group started by Cardinal Cardin. They would be always going off to meetings, and invariably bringing home members of their group for coffee, barbecues and parties that went on till all hours. As time went by, I couldn't help but be impressed by the quality of the friendships that I saw amongst my sisters and their friends. There was a level of sincerity and a sense of belonging that was all too lacking amongst my own peers. Although I maintained a cynical outer front towards these folks, internally they were giving me a lot to think about.

One day one of my sisters asked me to zip her into town on the back of my motor scooter. She was going to a 'house Mass'. This was something pretty much in vogue in the seventies. People would sit around on a lounge floor and, in a relaxed but very personal way, celebrate Mass. As we journeyed into the city on my bike, a battle raged within. Should I ask my sister if I could go with her to the Mass? I had to swallow my pride, as I had been very rude to her about her Christian friends. She could hardly contain her elation when I asked and welcomed me to join her. I remember it vividly to this day, as I sensed the presence of God at that Mass and it made a real impact on me. Everyone sang and prayed with sincerity and enthusiasm. There was something good happening and I knew I was on the outside looking in. As I sat there, I determined in my heart that whatever it was that I was sensing, I was going to get it. God saw the desire of my heart and I was not to be disappointed. This was a significant first step in my walk with the Lord.

I became increasingly involved with the YCW group, attending all kinds of meetings and get-togethers, which always involved an element of prayer and Scripture-reflection, as well as a tremendous amount of fun. During those first months I started to discover prayer. I would sit in a church and just talk to the Lord. He was becoming very real to me.

Eventually, our YCW group came into contact with people who were involved in something called the 'charismatic movement'. I was at a party when a friend asked me to go for a walk. We climbed one of Wellington's hills and sat at the top overlooking the

lights of the city. He started to tell me about the charismatic movement, about people who had experienced the
Holy Spirit in a radically new way. We talked about,
'speaking in tongues' and 'prophecy'. It all sounded
completely strange, and yet at the same time I was
stirred and willing to explore. We ended up going to a
prayer meeting, and then being invited to do a 'Life in
the Spirit' seminar.

At this time, the Charismatic Renewal was very new
in New Zealand, and there was only a handful of people
involved. We would gather for Mass early on a Saturday
morning in the centre of the city, and then go to a friend's
house where the Life in the Spirit seminar was being
held. Each week there was a talk and then a small group
discussion. In addition, there was the booklet which
gave us a Scripture passage for each day to reflect upon.
My relationship with the Lord grew immensely at this
time. I started to experience that not only could I talk to
God, but that he wanted to talk to me. I hungered to get
away for those times of prayer. The Scriptures started to
read like a personal love letter. This was a tremendous
awakening. We started to meet other folk who were a
part of this charismatic movement and then went to conferences where we heard international speakers who
were experiencing the same reality of God in their lives.
Always there was this dramatic theme of life, life in
abundance. It was incredibly exciting.

We started to hear about the formation of charismatic communities, where people who had this experience
were coming together, committing themselves to one
another, and establishing a common life together. This
seemed to be a very natural step, and so we decided to
form a Christian community. We didn't have too much
experience in these things, which is probably one reason
why we had the nerve to attempt it in the first place!

There were about fifteen of us when we first came
together, eventually growing to around twenty-five. We
had two separate households, one for single men and the

other for single women. It was a tremendous experience, although not without considerable difficulty and trials. However we certainly all grew through it. We lived in community for a couple of years and then reached a point where we had not the experience or wisdom we needed to advance to a further stage and so we put it to rest.

Like many New Zealanders, living at the far end of the world, I had a growing desire to travel. I wanted to see a bit more of the world and I wanted to visit some of the communities in other countries, about which we had been hearing so much. I recognised that my faith was still not overly strong and that I could easily be buffeted by doubts and the attractions of a worldly lifestyle. I was therefore keen to find a place where I would be encouraged and helped to grow in my faith. I was working at the time as a probation officer for the Justice Department, having earlier completed a university diploma in social work. I sensed that God had some kind of full-time ministry for me but I didn't feel called to the priesthood. In 1982, I left New Zealand and headed off for what New Zealanders call 'OE', overseas experience. I visited charismatic communities in Australia and then in England, before starting on a bike tour of Europe. I cycled several thousand miles through Norway, Sweden, Denmark, Germany and Holland, before finally stopping at the Castle Croy community whose address I had, in the south of Holland. I was welcomed warmly, as we had a mutual friend in New Zealand.

Also staying at the Castle Croy community at the time was a Youth With A Mission team. I had once read a book by Floyd McClung, one of the senior leaders of YWAM, but had had no real contact with this mission organisation. What immediately impressed me was how open and down-to-earth the people were and, at the same time, how real and how solid was their love for God. Their community lifestyle struck me as balanced and full of celebration. I made it a point to corner differ-

ent members of the team alone and question them closely about YWAM and was quite impressed with what I
heard and observed. I then started to hear about something called a Discipleship Training School, which is the
basic training unit of YWAM. Some of the folks from the
Castle Croy community, who had already been through
a Discipleship Training School, were going to go to Spain
to help staff another school, but this time it was to be a
school especially geared towards Catholics who were
interested in lay missions.

I spent a while considering and then, sensing God's
leading, decided to go and do this five-month training
school. It was wonderful, and again a time of deepening
my walk with the Lord. It was then a very natural step to
join the staff and work with YWAM. I worked with
Bruce Clewitt, who was at the time leading YWAM's
work in Austria. Bruce had been key in helping YWAM
grasp the challenge of working with Roman Catholics.
YWAM from the outset has been an interdenominational grouping, but for the most part had drawn its staff and
students from the Pentecostal–Evangelical–Anglican
world. Bruce, with his experience in Austria, pioneered
an approach of serving and collaborating with Catholic
charismatic groupings. This approach has become widely accepted within YWAM. In the last two years we've
launched a ministry under the umbrella of YWAM called
'Kerygma Teams', which particularly seeks to be a
vehicle for young Catholics wanting to get involved in
contemporary lay mission work.

I continued on the staff with YWAM in Austria for a
number of years, working alongside Bruce, and then, in
1987, I moved to Ireland, where I took on the leadership
of YWAM, working from their base in High Park
Convent, Gracepark Road, Dublin 9. The Lord was very
good to me – in the months after I arrived I got to know
the most wonderful Irish girl and we married in 1989
and now have five children, including our latest offspring, twin boys, who are currently two years old. Our

work here in Ireland is primarily directed towards
young people. We run school retreats, and are involved
in helping to launch and support a number of youth
groups in parishes around Ireland. We have three cen-
tres: one in Dublin, one in Charlestown, Co Mayo and a
third in Banbridge, in Northern Ireland. We have a total
of forty-two full-time staff, with fifty per cent of them
being Catholic Christians.

I am also involved in 'Relay', an initiative amongst
Catholic charismatic leaders, working in the areas of reconciliation, evangelism, lay ministry and youth. As I
look over my life, I can see God's hand very clearly. My
personal relationship with our Lord Jesus Christ has
become the rock on which my life is built. I seek to grow
in that relationship each day as I pray and read Scripture.
I am grateful for the rich heritage I have in the Catholic
Church. My life has also been enriched by my many
Protestant and Pentecostal friends with whom I work
and fellowship.

4

JESUS IS ALIVE!

REV DONAL GODFREY S.J.

*Rev Donal Godfrey is a Jesuit Priest in Belfast,
involved in reconciliation work.*

I was born in Liverpool in 1959. It was the same week
that a new Council was convened in the Roman Catholic
Church. Pope John XXIII asked for a 'new Pentecost' and
I am happy to be living in a time when such a revival of
faith is actually taking place, in all the Churches. I was
brought up as a Catholic in a neighbourhood where faith
did not seem to be very important for most people. In
fact we were considered rather odd because we actually
went to church each week!

My parents both worked as doctors. I am grateful for
their love. It is hard to know that God loves you without
first having had an experience of human love. Mrs
deBeire, the woman who looked after us each day until
my mother came home, often dropped in to the nearby
Catholic church with us, even though she herself was a
Protestant. I always appreciated the quiet and peace of
the church, and came to feel a sense of the reality of God
as an ordinary part of life.

My parents sent me to a boarding school called
Stonyhurst College. It was run by Jesuit priests. I was
interested in discovering more about God, and became
part of a prayer group in the college. After leaving
school, my family moved to Cork. I went on to study law
in Cork University and had an exciting time during my

three college years. I became president of the college debating society, revelling in the cut and thrust of debating contests.

It was at the end of my law degree that I became depressed. Life seemed to lose its meaning for me. Somehow I came to think that I was completely unlovable and unworthy. The Church appeared to me to care only about rules and regulations and I did not feel it could be of any help to me in my crisis. I could find no way out of my depression. I knew I needed help, but didn't know where to get it. Then I met a visiting American, who was an evangelical Christian. Sometimes it's easier to confide in a stranger. Doug helped me to see that being a Christian was not about working at pleasing God by my own efforts, but rather about surrendering to Jesus as my personal Lord and Saviour. I thought about it and decided that I would trust in Jesus as my personal Saviour and see if He would help me.

I experienced a sense of God's love for me in a completely new way. I had found a new beginning and a new life. In Jesus I now knew that I was loved and accepted exactly as I was. I could do nothing to earn this love, and I didn't have to change myself first in order to merit this love. I had discovered a personal relationship with Jesus. I simply had to accept His love for me as an unearned gift. Jesus entered the most intimate and vulnerable part of my very self and was able to console me and help me to see that He had plans for me. My life had meaning in the scheme of things. I have lost contact with Doug, but I always thank God for using an evangelical Christian to help me, a Roman Catholic, experience Christ in my heart in a new way

Billy Graham says, in his book *Peace With God*, that the life which comes from new birth cannot be obtained through self-effort. I now experienced this new birth, which is always God's work. I became very involved in inter-church and Catholic charismatic prayer groups, where I realised that God had more to give. I experienced what is called the Baptism in the Spirit, and found that my prayer life was deeper and more joyful. I also found in myself a great hunger for Scripture.

At this time, I encountered Christians from other traditions through the Full Gospel Businessmen's Fellowship meetings. I remember listening to Fr. Bob MacDougall speak of how God is not an idea or a theology or a philosophy . . . He's alive and real and His name is Jesus. That was, and is, my understanding of God. God is found and experienced in Jesus. Jesus is my companion, my friend. Like any human relationship, this one has changed and grown over the years, and it remains my primary relationship.

I began to sense that the Lord might be calling me to the priesthood in my own tradition. I wished this nagging sense would go away so that I could get on with my life as a barrister. Eventually I decided that I had better try it out, in order to get such feelings out of my system for good! Now, many years later, I am an ordained priest. I am also a member of the Jesuit order, which was founded by St Ignatius of Loyola. In Northern Ireland, where I live with a small community of Jesuits in Belfast, the name Jesuit seems to engender mistrust among some people. I have listened to Rev Ian Paisley, and read comic books from Chick publications that say things about Jesuits that are so far from the truth and so hurtful that it is very hard to know how to even begin a loving dialogue. Ignatius was a younger contemporary of Martin Luther and, in many ways, was like Luther in that he wished to revitalise the Christian faith by returning to the source of Christianity, i.e. Jesus. As part of my Jesuit training I did the 'Spiritual Exercises' of St Ignatius – over thirty days of silence. During this period, I realised that Ignatius desired Jesuits and other Catholics to have a profound conversion and a real experience of the Lord by accepting Christ as Lord and Saviour. Ignatius took the content of the Exercises from the life of Christ in the Scriptures.

There are four sections called 'weeks'. The first week is on the theme of creation and the disruptive effect of sin on the harmony of creation. I wrote a prayer in my journal: 'O Lord, come in the stillness. Let me bask in your light. Let your Spirit penetrate my depths, so I may be transformed. You made me in your image, help me to reflect you more each day, to love you more each day. All is gift, your gift, O Lord.'

In the second week we were led to meditate on the hidden life and the public ministry of Jesus; in the third week, on the passion and death of Jesus; and in the fourth week on the Resurrection. I experienced very different moods and feelings during this retreat, and I found it was possible to honestly express how I felt to Jesus. For me, Jesus is one who loves passionately and unconditionally. Although I do not always understand Him, He is one with whom I feel an intimate connection. Before Him, I can stand without shame or fear, revealing all my strengths and weaknesses.

In these Spiritual Exercises, Ignatius stressed that the Creator God deals directly with us, the created. The retreat helped me to see the ways in which this happens in my own life. In a way it confirmed, from within my own tradition, what I had learnt from my friend Doug, who first introduced me to Jesus as Lord and Saviour. Ignatius wanted to introduce people to Jesus as their personal Saviour. I understood that the best prayer takes place in the heart and not in the head. I still struggle with this, because it is often easier for me to stay cerebral rather than allow my prayer to be real, to come from my feelings and gut. For His part, I find that Jesus makes one demand, that I accept His love. This is harder to do than I ever imagined, because I tend to go looking for love in all the wrong places. Yet, when I am ready, He is still there waiting for me.

I have had to let go of false images that I have had of God. Some of these came from my upbringing and from what was presented to me by certain people within the

Church. Unfortunately, sometimes one is still given the impression that being a Christian is just a matter of duty, or of being respectable. Nothing could be further from the truth. Being a Christian is about an adventure, a life of risks, about having a personal and loving relationship with Jesus as Lord and Saviour. At times in this relationship, I have found myself expressing my anger and my resentments towards God. Often I have realised later that my real problem was that I had to get to know God better. I am still learning. This process can no more be exhausted than can any loving relationship with a friend. St Paul says we now see as in a mirror, dimly. In the next life, we shall see face to face.

The need for a personal encounter with Christ, as Ignatius proposed, is being rediscovered in our day in the Catholic Church. I can remember listening to Cardinal Suenens speaking at a charismatic conference in Dublin. Suenens spoke of the need to evangelise the vast number of nominal Christians within the mainline Churches. As he said: 'To be a true Christian means, furthermore, to have met Jesus personally, as Saviour and Lord. I must accept Jesus totally, as a reality, the Lord and Master of my life . . .' As Catholics, we have been sacramentalised, but often are not evangelised. We need to come to this personal experience of Jesus as Lord and Saviour.

I was privileged last year to be the first Catholic priest to be part of the organising committee for March for Jesus here in Northern Ireland. The committee would often meet for early prayer breakfasts in the Jesuit Community house, where I live. We need the enthusiastic kind of evangelisation exemplified in March for Jesus if our Church is once again to be fully alive in the Spirit. Jesus said that conversion is as radical as going back into your mother' s womb and starting all over again, being born again. Although I was born and raised a Catholic, I know I cannot be a Christian by birth, by custom, or by tradition. I can only be a Christian by deciding to choose

Christ, and accept Him into my heart. Christians are those like Peter who say, 'Lord to whom can we go? You have the message of eternal life.'

I realise now that conversion is, in some ways, a life-long process. I had the moment of accepting Jesus as my personal Saviour and that was a crucial moment. But I have discovered that Jesus invites me to ever new and deeper forms of conversion. He brings about intellectual, emotional, psychological and social conversions. Some years ago I lived in one of the poorest areas of Dublin, where unemployment is very high. Having been brought up in a very middle-class world, I soon discovered that I had a fair amount of prejudice about working-class people, like those in Ballymun. In actual fact, they had quite a bit to teach me! Living in Ballymun also helped me to see the need for social justice in the world. I saw the need to be both evangelical and socially conscious.

Jim Wallis explains this better than I can. He says that in both the Old and New Testaments, conversion involves a change of lords. Conversion from idolatry is a constant biblical theme. The people resist and cling to their idols. Our contemporary idols are wealth, pride of nation, power, etc. Every part of our lives stands in need of this conversion. The Bible sees conversion as being necessary for the erring believer, as well as for the non believer. To be converted to Christ means to give one's allegiance to His Kingdom. Our conversion is our point of entry to the Kingdom. Our own salvation, which begins with a personal decision about Jesus Christ, becomes linked with the fulfilment of the Kingdom of God. This connection is central, and I think I learnt this in Ballymun, and also in El Salvador, where I visited the site where Archbishop Romero was martyred.

Our Churches need to concentrate on this need for an evangelism that confronts each person with the choice about Jesus and asks if we will follow Him and the Kingdom. But our individual salvation cannot be separate from visible witness to God's Kingdom on earth. As a Christian I am called to do what Jesus did, that is, identify with the marginalised people in the world. Jesus is especially close to those who are excluded and oppressed. I saw this when I was depressed myself, because Jesus came close to me precisely where I felt oppressed and most vulnerable. I discovered this afresh one summer working in France with physically and mentally wounded people, at a community called L'Arche, which was founded by Jean Vanier. The first weekend, I was very frightened when someone threw a tantrum and started throwing chairs around. I panicked. However, gradually, these people taught me that God reveals His very self to the little and the wounded, to the extent that we accept that we are wounded.

Being reborn in Jesus is about surrendering to the power of the Spirit and allowing Jesus to take over. Each day is an opportunity to encounter Christ in my daily living and to listen to the ways in which He draws me to a deeper conversion.

After spending time in Ballymun, I was sent to Toronto in Canada to study theology. I was fortunate to be able to do courses in Protestant schools there and learn something of the rich traditions in other Churches. My Jesuit community was in an area of the city badly affected by the HIV virus, and a group of priests and lay people decided that some compassionate response was required. We began a monthly Healing Service for the HIV-affected community. It was most moving to be part of this service and I can truly say that I met Christ in the people that I came to know who were living with AIDS. I was then sent to San Francisco to do graduate studies in theology and in that city I also came across Christians who were living with AIDS. A while ago, I had a letter that read: 'Dear Fr. Godfrey, As a friend of Mr Arthur Diaz I want to inform you that he died on November 22 in Bonn, Germany . . . He often mentioned your help to Mrs Anna and him in the past . . .'

Arthur was a Christian and the only person who

cared for Mrs Anna, who was then in her nineties. He would bring her to the church where I was an assistant, even though he himself was not a Catholic. I would sometimes meet him for coffee and he was always joyful, dignified, and concerned for others even though he was suffering from full blown AIDS. He also suffered from discrimination because he was homosexual. However, Arthur spoke to me of his relationship with Jesus. I always felt that I was meeting Jesus in him. He gave me hope and, in a way, he was the one who ministered to me.

After finishing my studies in California, I returned to Belfast. I am still very much in contact with my brothers and sisters in Christ from evangelical backgrounds. Jesus has a very different priority from that of many of our Churches. He desires that Catholic and Protestant people come into a loving relationship with Him. Unless we are converted to Him, how can we ever come to accept, let alone love, each other? Christ opens up horizons that are inclusive of all our traditions, but I do not believe that He minds if we are unionist or nationalist, Catholic or Protestant.

I remember going to an inter-church service at the Anglican Cathedral in Belfast, and passing picketers outside, protesting against the visiting preacher, Cardinal Martini of Milan. There were many placards highlighting the fact that he is a Jesuit. I tried not to attract too much attention! However, one person gave me a leaflet which stated that neither the Catholic nor the Protestant Churches could save. I wanted to say how right he is, and that I completely accepted everything in his tract as true.

I know that I need to start by repenting of my own sectarianism. The Lord is calling us to a new understanding of ourselves that sets us free of our old ways of thinking. We need to see that being a Christian is a new way of being that has a much stronger demand on our loyalty than nationalism or unionism. In Belfast, I keep seeing murals that depict scenes sacred to one side or the other. God is usually invoked, as if God is always on the side being portrayed. But God refuses to be put into such an idolatrous box, for the Holy Spirit is blowing in the House Churches, in Pentecostal churches, in Protestant churches, and in Catholic churches. This spirit of revival will not be confined in the traditional categories. Differences between the Churches will remain – but even in New Testament times there were different theologies. There is, however, one Lord and one Saviour.

I believe that Jesus is alive today in my heart. I know and experience a deep unity with other Christians who know Him as Lord and Saviour. Jesus is alive and the God I believe in seems to turn up in unexpected places, both within myself and in the world.

5

'HANDS-ON' YOUTH WORK

ED CONLIN

*Ed Conlin is Associate Director of Youth Initiatives
in a deprived area of West Belfast. He has seen over 150
young people come to a living faith in Jesus Christ,
many of whom were joy riders, etc.*

My name is Ed Conlin. I was born in Detroit, Michigan.
I grew up as a Catholic in a city bristling with
black/white tensions, which erupted periodically in riot-
ing and burnings. We were forced to move house when
I was ten. I distinctly remember, on my first day in my
new school, feeling very close to God, as if Jesus had His
hand on me and everything was going to be all right. I
even made so bold as to reassure our nervous looking
young nun: 'Jesus had to flee his home too, and look how
everything turned out for him!'

My parents taught us that, as Catholics, we should be
tolerant towards all other people, that racism was
wrong. As I grew older, and especially in high school, I
often encountered the ugliness of it in unguarded com-
ments coming from people I had thought were 'ordinary
decent folk'. I was very active in sports and had a lot of
black friends. I was really glad I did on one occasion,
when a race riot broke out in our high school. I was
about seventeen at the time. In one day, several people
were knifed and there was $30,000 worth of damage
done. I came out of the science lab and ran into a mob of
black folk coming down the corridor with knives and

baseball bats. I remember just saying, 'Oh God, help me.'
I rushed into a toilet, thinking I'd stand on the toilet bowl
in one of the stalls and just hope they'd think it was
vacant. But there were two black guys standing in there,
one of whom had a knife. I thought that was it. Then I
recognised one of them. I'd played sports with him, and
we'd been in a car pool together, giving lifts to each
other. I looked at him and said, 'Give me a break, man.'
He just looked at his friend and said, 'Not this one, let's
leave him.' And then, just as the mob were bursting
through the toilet door, my friend pushed me into the
stall and pulled the door to. Some of the mob shouted,
'Any white honkies in here?' I just stood petrified and
this guy said, 'Get on, there's only us blacks.' So on they
went, to my inexpressible relief. I felt the mercy of the
Lord and I also felt that He had underlined for me the
importance of tolerance and mutual care. It was a deeply
formative experience for me. I knew God was asking me
to give to others, to be tolerant and understanding and
that such a way of life would bring His blessing.

In my high school years, I very much enjoyed the fun
of being an irresponsible teenager, though I experienced
a fair bit of tension in my final years, as drugs came into
our school. A lot of my friends were experimenting with
them and I felt under pressure to follow suit. I did experi-
ment a little, but never felt right about it. Then, in my last
year of high school, I was playing football with a black
guy who was a Baptist and who had experienced conversion. He was a very good football player and we had
a good relationship. We respected each other. But I was
really taken aback when I first found out that he was a
Christian. One day, he started telling me about how he
prayed to Jesus and how Jesus was a friend to him. As a
Catholic, I had had a close awareness of Jesus with me
when I was young and I'd lost it as I'd grown older and
my life had become more sophisticated. I really sensed
this was what I had been missing. I had lost track of
Jesus. I heard this Baptist football player talk about his

faith in the Lord and it just pierced my heart. I felt Jesus calling me back to Himself. The faith I had had at ten wasn't enough for my eighteen-year-old mind, which was awakening to new desires, new concepts and new moral challenges. But I felt that Jesus was coming back to me, as an adult, and saying, 'OK now, I'm still here.' It really hit me that I was on a path with Him and that path was going to lead me ever closer to Him.

My friend led me in a prayer of life-surrender to Jesus. For me, this was a significant step in my journey into Christ. I was on the path again. I was right with God on my journey of faith, with the Church providing, as it were, stepping-stones and signposts along the way. But my personal relationship with the Lord was, and is, the most important thing.

The change of direction that I experienced in this prayer was encouraging, but somewhat frustrating. Drugs, drink and sex were the norm in my high school and at times the pressure was difficult to withstand. I experienced the embarrassment, the frustration and the inadequacy of not being able to live out the Christian life as I knew I ought. Fortunately, I met a man named Jim Bertoluchi, who was a member of a charismatic community called the Word of God and who also knew my Baptist friend, Gary. I talked with him about my inability to live the life I wanted to live and he encouraged me to do a 'Life in the Spirit' seminar. That experience was a real eye-opener for me. First of all, I came to clearly recognise my own state, to realise I couldn't do anything to better myself. I lacked the power, the will power as well as the grace. Receiving the sacraments was important to me, but didn't give me experiential power to overcome my sin. Then Jim led me in a prayer for the Baptism in the Spirit – to receive a fuller outpouring of the Holy Spirit in my life. I believed that I had received the Spirit at baptism, but, as a child, I had no real understanding of my need to yield myself fully to Him, to have my whole life infused by Him. Now I knew, from sad experience of personal failure, my great need for the empowering of God in my life. In the weeks that followed, I began to experience changes in my attitudes. I had a stronger desire to be with Christians. I noticed a certain kind of will power in me that I hadn't had before. I experienced the fruits of the Spirit working themselves out in my life, God's character emerging in me, His child. I received the gift of tongues and I experienced spiritual grace for service and, in particular, for working with young people.

University was a tough time. The university I attended was especially infamous for its immorality. I believe it was the grace of Baptism in the Spirit that brought me through that time. I knew that I was there by God's call, to serve His people, to speak the Word of God in that situation. The knowledge that I was there to bring light gave me strength to resist temptation. I felt that I had a purpose and a mission. I wasn't just cast adrift in an immoral situation, but I was really placed there by God and His grace would be sufficient for me.

I graduated from university and went to Brussels, to work with Cardinal Suenens. I had been involved with a group of men called The Servants of the Word, an order of brothers who came from both Catholic and Protestant backgrounds and felt a call to live in unity. They also had a call to mission work, especially to speak the gospel to young people. Some of them, including Ralph Martin and Steve Clark, were working with Cardinal Suenens, to help start a charismatic community in Brussels. I learned French and Flemish, so that I could work with the young people. I worked there for six years, knowing real blessing in the service of God and experiencing the joy of encountering the wider Body of Christ in Europe.

I was then asked to go to London, to be part of a team working with university students. It was an exhilarating experience, working with the different denominations in the seventeen universities in London. After five years, the leaders of a charismatic community in Belfast, called

Community of the King, which numbered about 450 adults and children, invited me and two others to come and work with young people in Belfast. I came over with Jamie Treadwell, an Anglican, and Bret Lockhart, a Presbyterian. From this youth work grew Youth Initiatives, a charitable trust, established in 1991, co-founded by Jamie and myself.

We work with thirteen- to twenty-one-year-olds, and are currently experiencing quite a stretching of our resources. There's just always more to do than is possible. We've grown to a staff of eleven and have forty young volunteers. These volunteers have the privilege, and the challenge, of working for the discipleship, training and formation of the younger age group. They serve alongside the team members, and learn as they go along. We have a whole programme set up for the volunteers, enabling them not only to learn how to work with young people, but also how to bring them into deeper relationship with Christ.

We find if we don't work with the boys when they're thirteen or fourteen, they're very difficult to reach at a later stage. So we have programmes that are fairly intensive: evangelistic programmes involving sports, drama, music, service projects, boys' challenge projects etc. We do a lot of outdoor activities. Our aim is to get them involved, right from the start, in a positive peer environment. Here, they are not only protected from the drink and drug problems and the paramilitary threats, but they also learn from their observation of committed young Christians who are just a few years older than themselves, as well as from teaching input at weekly prayer meetings, which most of them attend. Even so, a lot of boys drift away at the age of fifteen or sixteen and we find that a big challenge. They lack the moral fibre to stick with the commitment or to stand up against their friends when they get ridiculed for not showing their manhood. We work with probably a few hundred teenagers, both boys and girls, and we have a lot of opportunity for them to serve, because we've developed a fairly extensive programme in drama and music. We have three bands and a drama team that have engagements in different venues almost every week. We have a lot of service projects in the local community, and outside. We have boys' and girls' programmes. They have their own small groups, where they have a chance to hear input relevant to their own particular struggles. Then we have a weekly prayer meeting to which all the young people are invited. Around a hundred attend. They are clearly prayer meetings, with the explicit aim of finding more life in Christ, but with the added enjoyment of drama, music and crazy games.

One of the things we've come to realise is that the young people need to feel they have a contribution to make. If they think they haven't, they lose self-esteem and they get into anti-social behaviour very quickly. We've found that the huge estates of Poleglass and Twinbrook, with their thousands of children, provide us with a brilliant opportunity. We run a summer scheme, where our teenagers help out with running camps for eight- to thirteen-year-olds. We also run community nights, for all age groups, and a parents' night, where we do dramas for the parents and games for their kids and have tele-tubbies and costumes, and Barneys all over the place. We run different services in the community, house-decorating projects, tidying up gardens – tearing down walls and fences. The boys especially love to tear things down! We try to do that constructively. We do quite a bit of service in the parish, helping out with a youth group, a music group and a monthly Youth Mass.

It has been a challenge to keep all these activities running, but it seems that the way that young people understand their self-worth is in making a contribution. We also find that the average young person starts with us about thirteen or fourteen and, if he or she does well, continues until eighteen. But about that age, if they have not begun to give back something of what they have gained by way of service to the younger people, then they seem to find themselves unable to persevere in the Christian walk. At that age, they are finding the challenges of drink, drugs and sex very strong, and that's when they need to make a stronger commitment to an alternative lifestyle. It's very difficult to get them to do that. They may be thrilled at a conference or at a summer camp where they experience the Lord and make a commitment, but if all their friends are drinking, their parents are both alcoholic and there's domestic violence at home, then it's very hard for them to stand against the tide. We try to provide a positive alternative environment. I would say it works sometimes, but often it doesn't. Twenty per cent of the young people probably make it. Eighty per cent don't and that's a painful statistic for me, because it's not just a statistic. I can see the faces of several hundred young people who, as far as we can see, didn't make it.

Probably sixty to seventy per cent of the young people we serve either don't know their fathers, or their fathers aren't living at home, due to imprisonment or some other reason, such as alcoholism. I find myself very involved in their daily struggles and crises. The sociological deprivation in our area is the highest in Northern Ireland, with seventy per cent male unemployment in Poleglass. This opens the door to all kinds of damage in the lives of these young people. And they're just gold, rough diamonds in the midst of a chaotic situation. It's glorious work, but it costs! These young people are not just clients to me. They're my own family. I love them.

That's where I struggle with hope. I see this society's not getting better. I see the world, with its enticements, really getting stronger. There are not many grounds for great joy, but on the other hand, I know there is a Source of hope and I do see a lot of young people find new life. So I pray daily for the courage to keep doing this work. I experience it as a challenge. I know in my heart of hearts that the Lord has a plan for all these young people. I may not see them blossom – I may see them get buried – but maybe in the future they'll blossom into a beautiful tree for God. For now, I have to keep my eyes on God's call to me, and draw quite a bit on the support of my brothers and sisters on the team. We struggle, all of us, with the failures and the successes, with holding on to our faith in the Lord.

The team consists of six Catholics and six Protestants. Some of the younger team members have come up 'through the ranks' of the youth work, and we've been able to employ them full-time. Some of the others – James, Doug and myself – are Servants of the Word, full-time missionaries. The wonderful fellowship we experience in the team is one of the highlights of our service. We really do have to support each other through difficult situations, and our experience is that God has been good to us.

We have a pretty clear understanding of our approach to evangelism. Some tensions arose early on when, at a camp, some of the Protestant leaders led the kids in a commitment to Christ and then, when the kids got home, they experienced confusion from their parents and an angry reaction from some of their acquaintances. They also found they were unable to live out their commitment at that age of fourteen or fifteen years old. We've since talked a lot about conversion and about the key elements in it which both Catholic and Protestant can agree upon. We work from a basis of conversion and growth, seeing it as a process. Both are necesssary – a decisive moment of commitment, but also growth and support in the living out of that commitment. We don't try to build up the kids to expect that, now they've made their commitment, they are going to float through life to Heaven. We tell them that this is a beginning, which is going to demand a full-hearted commitment from them, but that God will give them the necessary grace, and we will provide them with a strong support network.

As Youth Initiatives has developed, we have seen a

lot of our young people having quite an impact for reconciliation in Northern Ireland. A number of Protestant churches have invited them to come and minister in music and drama. They've been very impressed by the genuine faith of the young people. You don't sit down with a teenager and argue about doctrines, but you see the life in him, you see him pray and you see his enthusiasm for Christ and that disarms a lot of people who would have traditionally stood in fear of what Catholics represent. This interdenominational witness has been one of the most powerful witnesses Youth Initiatives has had over the years. Part of the impact derives from the fact that the young people have had to overcome so much to be there at all. They're keen to be there. They really do love to serve and they don't see a lot of doctrinal problems with going to Protestant East Belfast to do a drama to express their faith. It wouldn't have been in their background to see the divide as a conflict between Protestant and Catholic doctrine. They would rather have seen it as a political thing – 'Brits out!' So, when they go into a Christian environment they just see in the Protestant congregation their brothers and sisters in Christ, nothing more. This to me is clear testimony to the work of Christ in their lives, to the triumph of the gospel. Knowing their individual backgrounds, it is for me a source of 'joy inexpressible and full of glory' (1 Peter 1:8).

6

A MEDICALLY CONFIRMED HEALING

SR. MARGARET MCSTAY C.P.

Sister Margaret McStay C.P. is a sister of The Cross and Passion Congregation who has worked most of her life in the field of education, in Africa, England and Ireland. She is a spiritual director in the Cursillo Movement and involved in the Catholic Evangelization Movement, retreat work, counselling and the Evangelical Catholic Initiative.
At the ecumenical level, she works alongside Rev David Jardine as Duty Director of the Interdenominational Divine Healing Ministries, bringing together for prayer Christians from different denominations .

I was born into a Catholic family where prayer, relationship with God and relationship with each other were given high priority. Personal and family prayer, attendance at church and the reception of the Eucharist were encouraged. This Christian upbringing bore fruit, for me, in an attitude of caring and compassion for others, especially the elderly and the lonely, whom, from an early age, I was sent out to visit and help.

My school days were happy and uneventful. I grew up in a 'mixed' area, having both Protestant and Catholic friends. But, on looking back, I recall that we were not unaware of differences and prejudices. Lines of some sectarian chants which young people exchanged during the month of July still spring to mind. However, apart from that month, when the Orange bands marched to commemorate the victory of the Protestant King William over the Catholic King James in 1690, we got along well together. Sometimes we discussed our different ways of praying and worshipping, but not in any argumentative way. I remember a special friend of mine, who was a Protestant, wanting to pray together with me. The problem was that we were not allowed to go into each other's churches, so where would we pray? We eventually solved our dilemma by deciding to meet in the graveyard! So many years later, what poignant overtones that memory has!

At the age of eleven, during a special Mission in our church, I was led by the Holy Spirit to commit my total life to God. With all my heart I reaffirmed the commitment to God made for me at my infant baptism. I invited God to take over my whole life. As a mark of my commitment, I decided I was going to go to Africa as a missionary sister. To my intense frustration, those with whom I shared my secret reacted with amusement. When I was sixteen years old, I took my first step in that direction by arriving home with application forms for admission to a missionary congregation. My parents did not think much of this bright idea, and I can still see myself, in bewilderment, putting the papers in the fire and watching my grand scheme go up in smoke. Nobody understood me. My dreams were shattered. I was a failure!

However, some time later, my father discussed the situation with me and pointed out that the family were really only concerned about my happiness. He suggested that I leave things for a few years, widen my circle of friends and give consideration to what I would be giving up by entering the convent. I reluctantly agreed. I had difficulty at first in moving out from a fairly close-knit circle, but as time went on, I began to enjoy a fuller life with sports, drama, dancing, cycling and many new friends. Time went merrily on and my life could easily have taken another direction, but for the fact that God continued to pursue me. I remember moments when, during an enjoyable social occasion, I would become gripped by a yearning for 'something other' and a sense of 'not belonging'. This sense of there being 'something else' for me haunted me. I began to wonder if there was something wrong with me.

This sense of dissatisfaction resulted in my setting aside one hour each night to pray in the church for guidance regarding what God wanted from me. I decided to set the terms by requesting God to let a light appear on the sanctuary wall if I was to be a sister! The instrument He used was rather more mundane, in the shape of the priest who was the spiritual director of our Youth Club. I bumped into him one night coming out of church and he remarked 'I've seen you praying a lot. I'm sure God must be speaking to you. What do you think He is saying to you?' That night I went home and opened my heart to God as never before and came to a settled conviction in my heart about the path He wanted me to follow. In September of that year, despite pressure from many quarters not to go to 'the nunnery', I joined The Sisters of the Cross and Passion.

This is an international congregation. Inspired by the passion, death and resurrection of their Lord Jesus Christ, their prayer and work is animated by the desire to draw others into the experience of the compassion of Jesus. The sisters take vows of evangelical poverty, chastity and obedience and commit themselves to a community life of prayer, study of Scripture, worship and service of the poor, the powerless and the marginalised.

My probation period, from September to April, was a real spiritual honeymoon time of basking in the joy and love of God. My family came to see me being officially received as a novice and I was fortunate to be able to spend a good deal of time alone with my father, whom I dearly loved. He had always considered me very independent, to put it mildly, and was anxious to find out how I was coping with the structureed conformity and obedience required in the cloistered life. He was so delighted when I assured him of my happiness.

That night, when my family left, I started to weep bitterly and uncontrollably, causing great concern to the other sisters. I had not shed a tear since arriving at the convent, and they wondered if I was having regrets about the step I had taken that day. When I told them that I knew that I would not see my father again, they tried to reassure me, saying that I was talking nonsense. But, sadly, my premonition proved right. My father died suddenly from a heart attack the following August.

My life turned upside down. I was swamped in grief, shock, denial, and guilt for not having stayed at home for a while longer before leaving to join the convent. In the regime of convent life in those days, one did not go home for funerals. To make matters worse, thinking that a 'good nun' did not talk about her personal pain, I foolishly tried to cope by putting on an efficient smiling face in public and weeping my heart out in secret. I anguished about my mother. How would she cope with the younger children? Should I leave the convent and go home to help her? She insisted that she wanted me to remain in the way of life to which God had called me, but I still felt guilty, agitated and unsettled. My big question was 'Why, God? How could You be so demanding when I have been trying so hard to give You my all?' The scripture I prayed regularly was that of Jesus in the Garden of Gethsemane 'Father not my will but Thine be done' – and then often added, 'But Your will is so difficult!'

My mishandled grief took a serious toll on my health and I was informed by my Superior General that I could not be considered healthy enough to go to Africa as a missionary. I swallowed my disappointment and prayed that I would be sufficiently physically fit to become professed as a Sister of the Cross and Passion, to serve God wherever He might place me. Deep down there was no doubt in my mind that He would answer my prayer and, three months before my profession date, He healed me.

After my profession, I settled easily into teaching, in a Lancashire school, and really enjoyed working with young women who were quite close to me in age. At this time I began to long for more spiritual vitality in my relationship with God. To my delight, Pope John XXIII opened the windows of the Church to the hurricane wind of the Holy Spirit by ushering in the Second Vatican Council. I sensed that the Jesus who said 'Behold I make all things new', was at work changing many aspects of the Church, removing burdensome rules and regulations and opening ways to a greater sense of joy in life. Traditional convent life was swept by a great impetus for change.

I was asked to do a degree, and opted to combine Divinity and English. I found my Divinity studies exhilarating. By now the reactionary Council of Trent theology was beginning to give way to the outward going, more free and open theological approach of Vatican II. I devoured the Documents on 'The Church in the Modern World', 'Revelation' and 'Ecumenism'. The Document on Revelation led me to undertake an in-depth study of the Bible that has proved a lifetime blessing for me. My thesis on 'The Document on Ecumenism' deepened my knowledge of other Christian Churches and provided opportunity to meet and work with people from all the main denominations in England.

I opted to do some teaching practice in a Church of England school and was on the point of being offered a permanent post on the staff of the Religious Department when God unexpectedly directed me, through a request from my General Superior, to go to Africa. Just two days after I discovered that I had been successful in my degree, I was asked to go to Botswana. Since I had been told, a few years earlier, that my health would not allow me to work as an African missionary, I was surprised and disturbed. I had become quite settled working in

England and didn't really want to suddenly get up and
go. However, God was teaching me that obedience to
His direction is the all-important key to the release of His
power through our lives.

At very short notice, I said my heart-rending
farewells to my family and friends, let go of my dreams
and headed off to Africa. God rewarded me, not only by
blowing open my narrow Northern Ireland mind-set,
but also by opening up for me a much wider field of
interdenominational Christian work.

While teaching in Mater Spei College, I was also
involved in organising leadership workshops for the students. At one of these, co-led by a Baptist church leader,
we experienced a unique outpouring of the Holy Spirit.
To the consternation of many on the mission, the outworking of this blessing continued in the daily lives of
the students who had received it. At about 4 a.m. each
morning, the local bird life and my young student
friends gleefully combined to disturb the sleepers' rest as
they joyfully sang a 'new song to the Lord'! I only began
to understand more fully what had happened to us when
I returned to Ireland and encountered the Charismatic
Renewal Movement.

My return was triggered by the sad news that my
mother had terminal cancer. Fortunately, she enjoyed a
remission of about eighteen months. I was able to go with
her to interdenominational Charismatic Renewal meetings, which were thriving then. We received 'baptism in
the Spirit' and the gift of tongues and this sparked off for
me a deeper, more vital relationship with God and my
fellow Christians.

My Superiors decided I should remain in Northern
Ireland, enabling me to be on hand for my mother. My
work was in second-level education, but after a number
of years, I changed course and completed post-graduate
studies in Pastoral Leadership. These studies proved a
watershed in my life and equipped me to venture into
new areas in the spreading of the Kingdom among peo-

ple engaging in adult education, especially women. I do most of this work in the Ardoyne area.

At this time, God gave another unexpected twist to my journey. Rev David Jardine, a Franciscan Brother and Priest in the Church of Ireland, asked me to join him in his work, a new venture called 'Interdenominational Divine Healing Ministries', based mainly in St Anne's Cathedral. I accepted the challenge and daily experience the special blessings Jesus pours out in response to the prayer of people gathered together across denomination-al boundaries. Every Monday night in the cathedral, the worship, preaching and prayer ministry are shared by Protestants and Catholics. People come from all parts of the Church and city. Weekly we witness people turning to God. Many receive inner healing and peace through the grace of Jesus Christ. We also have recorded a signif-icant number of healings, such as the cure of a girl from epilepsy and the complete healing of a man in the last stages of multiple sclerosis.

Three years ago I myself suffered a severe health cri-sis. My immune system seemed to go out of control and I developed a serious problem in my right eye. After numerous tests and examinations by a number of eye specialists, I was informed that I had a rare congenital eye disease called Best's disease. It was incurable and untreatable. The prognosis was blindness. All they could do was monitor the progress of the illness in the hope of learning something that might help towards a future breakthrough in the treatment of the disease. I was told that my right eye was affected, but it was only a matter of time before the condition spread to the other eye and 'the blinds would come down gradually'. I would be blind. I sat in complete devastation, as student doctors were ushered in to view this extremely rare ailment.

I left the hospital numb with shock, clutching the only help they could offer me – a magnifying glass with a built-in light. A deep depression descended on me, driv-ing me into a tunnel that was darker and more soul-

destroying than blindness itself. I would gladly have
departed this life. Robbed of my ability to pray in my
normal way, I could only stand before God in brokenness and frustration and ask Him to free me of the guilt
I felt at not being able to communicate with Him. There
seemed to be no way out. It was especially difficult for
me when some people questioned why I, a member of
the Healing Ministry Team at the Cathedral, was not
experiencing God's healing.

But in my sorry state, I was constantly upheld by the
prayer and care of my fellow team members. Week after
week they came to pray with me, and week after week I
felt inwardly ashamed at not being able to report any
improvement. They remained steadfast in prayer and
faith and, one night, I received the grace to kneel down
and surrender my eyesight to God. 'Blind or not,' I said,
'my life is in Your hands and my trust is in You.' Faith
came flooding into my soul and I knew that somehow
my healing had begun.

It was fourteen months after the initial diagnosis
when I went back to the Royal for a check-up on the
progress of the disease. The eye specialist asked me,
'Madam, can you see sufficiently to distinguish between
the elements of cutlery in your kitchen?' I told him I was
out driving the car every day. He was amazed. He made
a detailed examination of my eyes, then went out and
came back with the senior consultant. He in turn gave
me a thorough scrutiny and pronounced that the disease
had completely gone, leaving only two tiny 'burnt-out
scars' in my right eye. The other eye was perfectly clear.
There would be no need for him to see me again! I was
speechless with joy and thankfulness. God had answered
prayer! I went recently for a routine check and was told
that there was only one little scar remaining. What a
wonderful God we have!

I continue in the Healing Ministry at St Anne's
Cathedral, rejoicing to see God's healing power at work
among His people and learning that He is never outdone

in generosity. Daily, from 12.00 noon in the Cathedral, we lead prayer for the healing of our troubled and broken land, knowing that only God has the key to peace.

Looking back on my life thus far, I can gladly say 'I set You as a seal on my heart, my God'. He has blessed me and fulfilled my desires in unexpected, joyful ways that have surpassed all expectation. My prayer is that I may glorify and praise His name forever as I live in obedient service to Him, and in union with all my fellow Christians. Amen.

7

DO YOU WANT TO BE HAPPY?

MARK CUMMINS

Mark Cummins is an executive in FAS, the State Employment Agency in Dublin. Mark leads a Catholic Men's Fellowship and is active in promoting renewal in the Catholic Church.

My name is Mark Cummins. I'm married to Eilish and we have five children. Today I can say we are a family unit because of the intervention of Jesus.

I was brought up as a very traditional Catholic and, as far back as I can remember, I knew there was a God. As I grew up, I feared Him. I saw Him as an accountant marking down everything I did that was wrong. When it was my time to die, He would open up the Mark Cummins Account and I would be found guilty. That would mean no Heaven for me. So I knew that somehow I would have to earn my way there, but I could never really be sure that I was doing enough. I felt that even if I were to get confession in the last moments of my life, I still couldn't be sure of getting into heaven. So I lived in that kind of fear of God.

Inside of me was a great big hatred of England and of Protestants in general. I never saw Protestants as being Christians. What I knew was that I was in the true religion and those outside would certainly go to Hell.

As a child I was very nervous – quiet and shy, with a very bad stutter. My schooldays were one long nightmare, which I thought would never end. When I left school at fourteen I was a total wreck, because now, added to my religious dread, was a completely demolished self-esteem. There was a big empty void of nothingness inside. My future was blank. I was no good. Eventually I started work as a hand-loom weaver. After a time, I got a chance of becoming a gent's cutter within the clothing industry.

Then I met Eilish. We decided to get married and we moved to Galway, where we had our first child. We bought a house and began to put our roots down. Our second child was born. After three years, I was made redundant. This really reinforced the lack of self-confidence within me. For the next two years, I worked here and there all over Ireland, while Eilish tried to sell our house. Eventually she did and we finally settled in Dublin. As the years passed, we had twins, followed by our last child. These were difficult years financially, putting a great strain on our marriage. As a result, somewhere along the way our relationship got lost and we drifted apart.

By this stage, God played no part in my life. Each Sunday I would bring the children to Mass out of habit. Then I began to notice big changes in Eilish. She began to behave more pleasantly and seemed better able to cope. She told me the local priest had prayed with her and she had been touched by the Holy Spirit. This really got to me. I resented the softness and tenderness I saw in her. The more she changed, the more I wanted out. What I did not know was that Eilish had begun to get her friends to pray for me.

One evening I was at home babysitting and had just finished reading a book. As I walked into the hall, I noticed another book on the floor. My first thought was, 'Don't touch it. It belongs to Eilish.' The second thought was, 'Pick it up.' I did not realise that in that moment of time my whole life was balanced on a knife-edge. Another thought came, 'Just look at the name of the book. That can't hurt you.' The title read, *The Happiest*

People on Earth. I felt an urge to pick it up, but again came the warning thought, 'Don't! It's one of those books Eilish reads.' There was a battle going on in me. Then the word 'Happiest' lighted up for me. Another thought dropped into my mind, 'Don't you want to be happy?' 'Yes,' I said, and picked up the book.

I was hooked. I had taken the first step in a process of coming into line with God's purposes for my life. I began to read about ordinary men who talked about Jesus as if they knew Him personally. They spoke of the power of the Holy Spirit and the miracles that happened as they laid hands on people. This was mind blowing to me. I thought miracles happened only in Lourdes, or places like that. Then they talked about speaking in other tongues – what was that? But the biggest shock to my whole system was the fact that these people were all from different denominations. They were Protestants! It had never entered my mind that Protestants could have the Holy Spirit. By the end of the book, I wanted what these men had. Suddenly, inside me, something changed. I was healed of my animosity towards Protestants. I felt the love of God flow through me for them. My only worry was, would I ever get what these people had experienced? I asked Eilish what I should do. She said, 'Pray!'

Time passed. Nothing seemed to happen. Then a neighbour called at my door and invited me to a Full Gospel Businessmen's Fellowship Meeting. I agreed to go. That was the 7th January, 1984. They started to sing songs to Jesus and the words melted my heart. One line I will never forget: 'He poured in the oil and the wine.' In the course of that meeting, I experienced right in front of my eyes everything I had read about in the book. I was very excited. Then the speaker called for anyone who wanted to give their lives to Jesus to come up to the front. I went up and was asked, 'What do you want?' I said, 'Everything. Whatever God has for me.' They laid hands on me and it was as if a fire went through my body. I burst out speaking in tongues. When I went home that evening, my marriage was totally healed. Eilish and I now have a new relationship. Only God's power can do that.

I was a member of the Full Gospel Businessmen's Fellowship for ten years. Then, after much prayer and discerning, I became convinced that God wanted me to work within the Roman Catholic Church, to reach men for Christ. I wanted other men to have what I had received. I wanted them to know Jesus as Saviour and to experience the fullness of life He promised us.

As I prayed, I received a name from the Lord: Emmaus. This was to be the name of the men's group I was to form. I prayed about a meeting place, and the name of a convent came to mind, the Disciples of the Divine Master Convent in Stillorgan. I asked for a specific day when we would meet and Thursday came clearly to mind. After much prayer, I went to the convent and there I met a Sister Paul. I asked her if there might be a meeting room available. She told me that at a meeting in the convent the previous evening they had felt they ought to have a men's group added to the various groups that were already using the convent facilities. She went on to say that she knew what name the group should have: Emmaus! It transpired also that the only night available was Thursday. So, on the 15th September, 1994, the first meeting of the Emmaus Men's Catholic Fellowship took place.

The Fellowship now meets every week in Coolock, in the north of the city. We meet to pray, read Scripture and share with each other our inward journeys. We see God changing men's lives. We see something of the Body of Christ in action. Each year we have an All Ireland Men's Weekend Retreat, open to everyone.

The Fellowship is active in outreach, running Life In The Spirit seminars and holding monthly meetings in Stillorgan. We have also engaged in a twelve-week outreach in Baltinglass, Co. Wicklow. Our desire is to bring

the Good News of Jesus Christ to our nation. The Holy
Spirit is working in our Church today, especially
through men whose lives have been transformed by
Jesus. It is His Church. We are part of His Body. What we
learn as we fellowship together, we seek to put into
action in our homes, in our parishes, in our work places.
We experience the reality of Jesus living and working in
and through ordinary men like us. We have come to
know what the two disciples on the way to Emmaus
experienced, when they said of their walk with Jesus:
'Were not our hearts burning within us . . .?'

8

EVANGELICAL: COMPLIMENT OR INSULT?

REV CIARAN DALLAT

*The Rev Ciaran Dallat from Jordanstown is the
Catholic Chaplain to the University of Ulster.*

When I was first called an evangelical by my
Presbyterian colleague in the chaplaincy at the
University of Ulster in Jordanstown, I wasn't sure
whether it was meant as a compliment or an insult!
Unfortunately in Northern Ireland a word like 'evangelical' can be loaded with colloquial meaning and, to
someone coming from the Catholic community, it often
is very negative. He explained what the word actually
meant and I discovered that I had been complimented.
However, to me it was just a new way of describing the
self-expression, the lived experience that seems always
to have been a part of me.

My name is Ciaran Dallat and I am the youngest of
seven children: two boys, four girls and then me. I grew
up in the small town of Ballycastle on the North Antrim
coast. My father was a schoolteacher and my mother
died when I was two. My father remarried and my new
mother is really the only one I have known. We moved
house when I was seven and most of my memories of
home are after that time. I loved where we lived, just
around the corner from the school and the chapel and
not too far to walk to the sea.

God was part of every aspect of daily life. Home, school and parish were so much part of each other. My father liked to go to Mass daily, as did my mother, albeit at a different time. Each day he woke us in order that we could go with him before we went to school. We were wakened at 7.30 a.m., went to 8 o'clock Mass, came home, had breakfast and then went to school. By the time I was nine, I was an altar boy. Being at Mass almost daily from the age of nine, I heard the Scriptures read many, many times and the teachings of Jesus were well known to me, if not always lived out!

I have five uncles who are priests and when they were home on holidays, or just visiting, it was always great fun to be in their company. They played hurling with us out the back, went for a swim with us at the Strand or just worked round the house. They were normal! The desire to be a priest was with me through those early years of my teens.

For my last three years at school, going to Mass each day with my father helped me realise something of the fact that it was in obedience to His Father's will that Jesus offered Himself in sacrifice for us. This realisation had a profound effect on me in that my being at Mass had grown out of me being obedient to my father's will and to the will of God. The necessity of being obedient to the will of God became a priority for me, a primary driving force for living.

As a student at Queen's University, I became very involved in the Folk Group at Mass, which used a lot of material based on the words of Scripture rather than the thoughts of hymn writers. This led me deeper into the writings of the Old Testament, particularly the psalms and the writings of the prophets. The desire to give more of my life to God grew stronger in me and so I entered the seminary in Belfast to train for the diocesan priesthood. I believed that God had a real personal love for me, and for others, and that I could help people become aware of that love and respond to it.

In the seminary we had plenty of time to learn to pray, to read the Scriptures and later to study theology. The unfolding of the Scriptures in our theological studies was a great source of nourishment to me for the life in relationship with God that I aspired to live. My teachers taught me how to read the Scriptures so as to discover the revelation God has put there about Himself, about what He has done for His people, about how they have responded and how He desires them to respond. From my study of the Scriptures I imbibed principles to live by, I received encouragement, challenge, direction and assurance of God's saving love in Jesus Christ.

As ordination drew nearer, particular passages became really important to me. I remember Philippians 2:5–11 being the main text in my prayer life in the whole run-up to being ordained a deacon. I was astounded at the incredible humility of Jesus, who 'being in very nature God, did not consider equality with God something to be grasped, but made himself nothing, taking the very nature of a servant'. What a standard for the ministry of a deacon!

As I approached priesthood, I kept coming back again and again to 2 Corinthians 4:1–10.

> Therefore, since through God's mercy we have this ministry . . . we do not use deception, nor do we distort the word of God . . . setting forth the truth plainly . . .we do not preach ourselves, but Jesus Christ as Lord . . . God . . . made his light shine in our hearts to give us the light of the knowledge of the glory of God in the face of Christ . . . we have this treasure in jars of clay to show that this all-surpassing power is from God . . . We always carry around in our body the death of Jesus, so that the life of Jesus may also be revealed in our body.

These words of Paul permeated my soul in the lead-up to ordination and set the tone for my priesthood.

The two years following ordination were spent in the parish of St Peter's in the Lower Falls, Belfast. It was a time of learning: learning to be a priest, learning about people, learning about politics, learning about the awful circumstances that so many endured and yet still remained faithful to God. I remember the joy of my first Christmas Eve when, after the celebration of the Mass for Christmas, as I stood outside on the steps of the church, the sense of belonging to the people of this parish over-whelmed me. I was overcome with joy at the realisation that I was linked with them by our common love for God, and that I had the privilege of being at their service in His service.

In August 1990 I got a shock: I was nominated as chaplain to the University of Ulster at Jordanstown. I arrived not knowing what I was to do, and found it to be a totally different type of ministry, not one that had been discussed at all in the seminary. I discovered that it was going to be whatever I made of it. I was coming from the structures of parish ministry, where I was part of a team of four priests working in harmony, to the unstructured life of university chaplaincy, where I found myself one of four ministers who were trying to learn how to work together. Some of the phrases I heard used to describe university chaplaincy indicated a ministry that was somewhat less than decisive: 'Walk creatively about the building!' and 'Loiter with intent!'

It was obviously going to take time to form relation-ships with staff, students and fellow chaplains.

The first term passed in a blur. It was early in the second term that I found in the story of the two disciples on the way to Emmaus a charter, or inspiration, for the ministry I wanted to live out. For me (and for some of the chaplains with me) Luke 24:13–35 has continued to be the model for ministry as a university chaplain. In imitation of Jesus, I try to 'walk' with our students and 'listen to their stories', try to help them 'understand the Scriptures' and when appropriate 'break bread with them' so that they can go and tell others that Jesus is alive!

9

I Shouldn't Be Alive Today

Jim Donnan

Jim is an executive with the Dublin Corporation and chairman of the Evangelical Catholic Initiative. He is involved with Scripture Union and the March for Jesus and leads Alpha Bible Study courses in his local parish.

Medically speaking, I shouldn't be alive today. My mother contracted a serious illness in her late teens and, when she got married, was strongly advised not to have any children. Despite this advice, she became pregnant and I was born, two months premature. I weighed just three pounds and spent my first six months in an incubator. My mother's health deteriorated over the months and she had to spend the next three years convalescing, while I was reared by my grandmother. Thankfully, she recovered, but my abiding childhood memory is of her poor health and a life of struggle. This in many ways reflected my early religious experience.

My image of God, growing up in a Catholic home, was of a distant God. I had a tremendous sense of sin and saw God as a taskmaster who was there to punish me, a policeman who monitored my every movement. In essence, I feared God and my goal was to earn His favour by doing good, in the hope that I might accumulate enough credit to get into Heaven. Despite all this there was a genuine respect for God in our home and I had a strong desire to serve Him in my life, at one time contemplating entering the priesthood.

In my teenage years I got involved in the Legion of Mary. When I was sixteen, I travelled to Scotland on lay missionary work with a small team and spent a week in a deprived tenement area of inner city Glasgow. Our task was to work in pairs and to knock on doors, inviting people to talk about God. Some people slammed their doors, some politely listened, while most were totally disinterested. But there was one notable exception. A dear old lady, Louisa Houston, lived alone in a cold bed-sit flat but warmly welcomed us in, almost as if she was expecting us, and kindly gave us tea. I was immediately struck by all the photographs mounted on the wall, each one having the person's name and a date recorded on it. She began to explain how she too was a missionary, but, as she spoke about Jesus her Saviour, there was a real sense that she knew Him personally, as if He was a real living person. Her expression brightened as she explained how the people in the photographs had 'come to the Lord'. She shared her faith in and love for Jesus in such a simple way, assuring us of her prayers. This amazing encounter was, in time, to totally change my life. I left Glasgow with a greater desire to serve God and a compulsion to help the poor.

I continued at school, but at weekends got involved in organisations like the St Vincent de Paul Society and the Simon Community. I also continued to correspond with Louisa who frequently shared a 'word from the Lord' with me. On leaving school, a group of around twenty school friends met regularly each Saturday to visit the old folks in Bru Caomhin, in Cork Street, Dublin. This had a social as well as a service dimension. One after-noon one of the lads, to our amazement, began to explain how he had met a girl in Grafton Street who told him how much Jesus loved him and pointed out to him in the Bible his need for salvation. Ray's attitude and character began to change and he wore out the pages of his New Testament with constant reading. With the zeal of a con-

vert he began to witness to the group. Some were quickly persuaded; others, like myself, resisted. But gradually,
one by one, all of the group committed their lives to
Christ.

Some began to fellowship in the Apostolic or Elim
Pentecostal Churches. I strenuously resisted the invitations to follow suit, despite the obvious change that had
occurred in the lives of my friends. However, I felt convicted of my need for Christ and when my girlfriend,
Barbara, now my wife, came into a personal experience
of the Lord, I felt compelled to pour out my heart to God.
I remember that particular evening. I simply knelt at my
bedside, beseeching God to sort out and take control of
my life. I asked for His mercy and forgiveness and invited Him into my life. There was no 'Damascus Road'
experience, but a great sense of peace invaded my life. I
had a complete assurance that my sins were forgiven and
experienced an immediate hunger for reading the
Scriptures. I wept as I realised for the very first time that
Jesus loved me personally.

I remember writing to Louisa soon after this experience, with a postscript, 'I enclose my photograph for
your collection'. Very soon afterwards, she replied. Her
letter was difficult to read because of the sheer excitement in which she expressed her praise to God for
answered prayer on my behalf. She explained how she
cried tears of joy at the good news of my coming to faith
in Christ. I am still amazed at how God should arrange
such circumstances to bring about my conversion.

While most of my friends started attending various
fellowships and subsequently left the Catholic Church, I
sensed a strong call to remain. I started attending a
charismatic prayer meeting in the Quaker Meeting
House in Eustace Street. It was a very exciting time to be
a young Christian as, week after week, the building was
packed with over 700 people of all denominations,
including Spirit-filled priests and nuns who gathered to
praise God and receive teaching. It was there that a life-

long friendship developed with a Quaker couple that I can best describe as my 'spiritual parents', Charles and Marge Lamb. Their love for the Lord, their hospitality and the very practical outworking of their Christian faith grounded on the Word of God, was a constant source of inspiration and encouragement. Barbara and I began to attend the weekly prayer meeting in their home and in this way God nurtured our faith and used this special couple to prepare us for Christian marriage.

We settled in Leixlip, Co Kildare, under what I believe to have been the guidance of the Holy Spirit, and opened our home for a weekly prayer meeting. We were blessed with two beautiful children, Paul and Sarah-Jane. While conscious of our own children's spiritual needs, we also began to focus our prayers on the needs of the parish and its rapidly growing population of children.

One summer, while on holiday, we heard of an evangelical Christian group running a Bible Club on the campsite. We were immediately impressed by the interest and enthusiasm of the children for the well-illustrated Bible stories and associated activities. We began to think, 'Could God do this in our parish of Leixlip?' With absolutely no experience or training, we explored the possibility of running such a club in a Catholic parish. Our incentive and inspiration came from Acts 14:27, which speaks of how God opened a door of faith to the Gentiles. We felt He was promising to open such a door of faith for us in Leixlip.

The parish priest gave his permission and the Board of Management allowed us to use the school hall. All we needed were the materials and some helpers. In another remarkable way, God brought me in contact with a respected Christian friend, Kingsley Prescott, the then General Secretary of Scripture Union. This contact was to have greater implications than the newly formed 'Good News Club'. Through the Scripture Union Family Weeks in Ovoca Manor, and elsewhere, my two children would have their lives changed.

Kingsley was remarkably helpful and supportive and provided us with Scripture Union Sunday School material. He also assured us of prayer at their daily staff meeting. Two of our friends, Marian and Brian Millar, kindly offered to help and soon the 'Good News Club' developed, with some weekly attendances exceeding seventy children. It continued for about six years.

My friendships and contacts with Christians from other denominations led to my involvement in helping to organise a number of 'Marches for Jesus'. I remember well the first March for Jesus held in Dublin, when some 10,000 Christians gathered. It was truly exciting to see Christians from various denominations, from North and South, walking side by side, lifting up the name of Jesus in song and praying for the nation.

Along the way, I developed a friendship with a man called Paddy Monaghan, which eventually led to the establishment of the Evangelical Catholic Initiative (ECI). This small group of Catholic Christians have been a real source of encouragement and fellowship as we work together on numerous conferences and reconciliation related initiatives.

More recently, our focus has centred on running Alpha Courses in the local parish. Alpha is a twelve-week course of clear biblical teaching, fellowship and social interaction. It is an amazing tool for evangelisation, and has been warmly commended by leaders in the Catholic Church. Of all the courses and meetings I have been involved in over the years, I can honestly say that Alpha has proved the most successful.

Our first Alpha Course was held in the home of Declan and Regina Slattery. The course was attended by eighteen parishioners, including two of the parish sisters and the local curate. A subsequent course was attended by up to forty parishioners, whose lives were greatly touched by the Lord, some now attending a fortnightly follow-up meeting. My strong desire is to see Alpha spread and be established in parishes all over Ireland.

Finally, as I write these words of testimony, I am so aware that what appeared to be chance encounters were indeed the loving and caring intervention of the living God at critical moments in my life. While still involved in the Catholic Church, He has sent Christians from many denominations to enrich and support my relationship with Him. This has strengthened my conviction that there is only 'one Lord, one faith, one body'. To Him alone be the glory, thanks and praise!

10

A NORMAL MARRIED LIFE

MARIE SCULLY

Marie is actively involved in the Evangelical Catholic Initiative and in promoting renewal in her church in Tallaght. She was also involved in setting up the Tallaght branch of the YMCA in Ireland.

I was born and raised in a home where both my parents were deeply committed Catholics. Yet I arrived at a stage where, married with one child, Cormac, and another on the way, I was very critical of the Church. I did pray and attend Mass, but would regularly criticise the sermons I heard. I was unsatisfied. Now that I was expecting our second child, I wanted to have something I really believed in to pass on to them. So I began to search for some answers.

At that time my husband, Joe, and I joined an Adult Faith Discovery Group in the parish. Two things stand out in my memory of that time. One was of the priest asking us to read the Gospel of St Mark. He was so nice and tried so hard to help us and to turn our group into a community, taking us walking in the mountains and getting us to have meals together, as well as helping us to study the Scriptures. So I tried to read Mark's Gospel, for the priest's sake. It bored me to tears. There was no change in my spiritual experience.

The second thing that I clearly recall was that one Thursday evening the discussion turned to God's covenant with Abraham. I found myself asking the question, 'Where is God's covenant with us today?' There was a silence and nobody answered me. Even the priest kept quiet. I thank God for that, because if, at that time, he had said something like, 'It's in Jesus Christ', I would probably not have pursued the matter any further. As it was, I had to continue my search.

I had our second baby. We called him Fergal. That summer, my brother, who was a priest, came home from Australia. He told us about a new movement sweeping the Church there. Then, through a priest friend, he learned that the same movement had just begun here in Ireland. He took us out to a prayer meeting in Finglas. This was an amazing experience. It was like arriving at a scene from the Acts of the Apostles. The house was full of people. They were sitting on the floor, on the window sills and on the stairs. I don't know how we found room to sit down. We were greeted like long lost friends. They were singing and praising God and my whole feeling was that whoever they were singing to, He was nothing like the Christ I had envisaged. It was wonderful and we went back a number of times.

My brother returned to Australia and my search continued. I heard about a prayer meeting in Eustace Street, the Quakers Meeting Place, and we decided to go there every second Friday. We enrolled in what was called a 'Life in the Spirit' seminar, which continued for several weeks. As part of this course, we were issued with a little booklet and asked to spend fifteen minutes in prayerful meditation on a different Scripture passage each day. About the third week of the seminar, the Lord began to move in my life. The talk that night was on the love of God. A young girl, about eighteen years of age, was giving the talk. She compared God's love to the love of a mother for her children, painting a lovely word picture of a young mother who was tireless in her attention to her baby's cries. 'No matter what time of the night the baby cried,' she said, 'the mother would jump up out of bed and run and take care of the child. This is how loving our God is.'

I was really annoyed at this description of God's love. I was a new mother and I loved my babies, but when my youngest, who was about two months old then, would cry in the night, my reaction was rather, 'Oh no, not again!' I would have to drag myself out of bed to go to him, or give Joe a nudge with my elbow and ask him to do it. I didn't want a God like me, who, when I called, said, 'Oh, no, not again!' That night on the way home, Joe said to me, 'Marie, you are really angry about this.' I said, 'Yes, I am. They're just dishing out a pile of rubbish to us. I go to Mass and get the same.'

The following morning, Joe took the boys to the library and I was left alone in the house. On the dining-room table I spotted the Life in the Spirit seminar booklet. I picked it up and and looked up to Heaven and said, 'This is it, Lord! This is the last time I'm going to do this! If nothing happens for me, that's it!' I went over and knelt down beside the armchair and opened the book. The reading for that day was Jeremiah 31:3 'I have loved you with an everlasting love and I am constant in my affection for you.' The words 'constant in my affection' stood out for me. I began to repeat 'constant affection'. The idea of being held in constant affection really moved me and I began to pray.

I don't know where the prayer came from, but I made an act of faith. I said, 'I believe Jesus died on the cross to save me from my sins. He even died to save me from my lukewarmness.' As I prayed, the room lit up. It was a wonderful light. It was as if I were in Heaven. I was praising God, singing at the top of my voice. I knew I was deeply and warmly loved and not only that, but I knew that He loved every single person in the whole world, even people like Hitler. As I sang and praised God, I sensed Him saying to me, 'Now get up and do your housework.' So I jumped up and began cleaning the house, singing and praising as I went about. I just knew I was loved and accepted and I wanted to run out and tell the whole world that God was absolutely madly in love with them.

The Lord began to teach me how to pray and gave me a wonderful love for Scripture. I went from being bored stiff with Mark's Gospel to being deeply in love with the Word. Tears would flow as I read it, especially St John's Gospel. It was like reading a love letter.

Joe and I began to attend the local prayer meeting and I was also invited to a prayer and Bible study meeting in a Quaker couple's house. This was a blessed time. Then we were invited to join the leadership of a local interdenominational prayer group, which grew to be quite large. After a time, a group of people within this meeting wanted to introduce the rosary and the Mass. We resisted this, because we believed that the Lord wanted to continue what He had initiated, a gathering of people from different denominations who were growing together as they prayed and studied the Scriptures together. I regret to have to say that gradually people from other denominations felt they had to leave and we were squeezed out of the leadership. This was a very painful time for us. While we went to occasional prayer meetings, we no longer attended any particular meeting on a regular basis. For about eight years, I progressed with the Lord in quiet prayer, while we continued to be involved in our normal parish activities and to hold a little weekly prayer and Bible study group in our own home.

Then five years ago, I attended a weekend, with a group of friends, in Roscrea Abbey. This was the beginning of an enormous further change in my life. The Lord revealed His living Presence in the Blessed Sacrament. A great healing took place in my life and I was gifted with an understanding of the Eucharist, which remains real for me today. I went back to the local prayer meeting and, once again, found myself very drawn to getting involved with reconciliation between the Churches. I was invited to join the Evangelical Catholic Initiative (ECI), an initiative for evangelism and reconciliation arising out of the declaration of a Decade of Evangelism in the Catholic Church. At one of our interdenominational leaders' conferences, the Lord showed me a picture of a small seedling, just barely above the ground. It was planted in very muddy waters. He told me that this plant of reconciliation needed to be nurtured. So began various little projects with this aim in mind. I was particularly encouraged by one such project, an 'open house' day entitled 'Who Is My Neighbour?' which attracted over fifty people, including our local priest, the local Church of Ireland minister and people from the Methodist Church and from some house churches. I also found myself calling a meeting of friends I'd known in the early days of the Renewal Movement, who had left the Catholic Church and formed house churches. We had some lovely times together, sharing the different paths along which the Lord had led us. I was invited onto the local YMCA Advisory Board and, through that, became a member of a YMCA cross-denominational working group. It has been a wonderful challenge. I'm still deeply committed to my own Church, especially my local parish, but look forward to continuing involvement in the process of reconciliation between the Christian Churches.

The Lord has continued to bless me. He has led me down paths I would never have thought possible. Right from the beginning, He put the unity of the Church on my heart and I love to meet with Christians from other denominations to pray and share what the Lord is doing in their lives.

Looking back twenty-two years, to the time when I invited the Lord into my life, I know I was, and still am, a very ordinary person. I didn't have huge problems. I wasn't a battered wife. I wasn't seriously ill. I just had the normal, everyday problems of a young married woman with two children. Asking the Lord into my life was the most wonderful thing that ever happened to me. Life has not been easy since, but it has been and still is, wonderful. I just want to give praise and thanks to our loving Father, whose desire to bless us is far greater than we can think or imagine. May the Name of Jesus be blessed now and forever. Amen.

11

WORKING WITH GOD

REV MICHAEL HURLEY

*Michael is a Catholic curate in north Dublin. He is the
founder of the cell-group movement in Ireland and
serves on the National Service Committee for
Catholic Charismatic Renewal.*

Early influences

It is a long journey from the rolling hills and green
valleys of West Cork to life in urban Dublin. It must
impose its own huge stress demands on the nervous and
emotional systems. I often wonder how I made the
transition. I have happy memories of growing up in the
1950s and 1960s. My family home was an open place,
where neighbours gathered at night-time to exchange
stories or to play cards. *'Muintereas'* ('sociability') was a
way of life. People were for each other. They went to one
another's assistance. They worked together at harvest
time. They were interested in one another, even if the
rivalry of success occasionally raised its head. I grew up
knowing that my parents wanted what was best for each
of us, their children. They had lived through very difficult times. They wished to give us opportunities which
they would have liked to have. Their options had simply
been emigration or remaining on the land. So education
was stressed as a pathway to new horizons.

The farmyard, where I saw the natural rhythms of
conception, birth, life and death, the green fields, marked
by seasonal changes, and school, where my bare feet

gingerly rested on musty boards and where we first competed on opposing football teams, completed the limits of life during my primary school days. It was a world with its own fields of exploration. The woodlands, the rivers, the lakes to swim in, the discarded pieces of timber to shape into an unwieldy hurley stick, transportation by motor car to play football in another village, these were all new worlds to be enjoyed and conquered. Din Joe, Paddy Crosbie and Michael O'Hehir, through the radio, were the only strangers invited into a sedate way of life.

Later came, for me, the seven-mile cycle each morning to secondary school. As I reflect back, I realise how deeply I still carry much of the environment of my childhood within me. I enjoy being with people. I believe that some degree of community is necessary for healthy living. I love the open air. New situations, events and ways of doing things fascinate me. Life, for me, is to be lived. It is not so much about argumentation, intellectual debates and great visionary planning. It is rather about getting on with the job in hand.

Until I was sixteen, there was very little to suggest that a life in the priesthood was for me. There was no great priestly line before me. God was not often spoken about in conversation. Faith was rather in the atmosphere in which we grew up. Sunday Mass, regular confession, and some formal family prayer, normally the rosary, were accepted as part of life. We took them for granted. We saw them as part of who we were. For all the lack of personal engagement, they gathered us together as a parish community, brought us to our knees as a family and provided a space for reflection as individuals.

Simple events evoke new horizons

One day, when I was sixteen, as I happily cycled through the countryside, I experienced what I can only describe as 'a surge of generosity'. It may have been the idealism of the 1960s. It may indeed be part of every young person's growth. In one instant I knew I wanted to do something worthwhile with my life. I wanted to make a difference. It seemed to me that it had nothing to do with religion. The strong impulse remained. I observed a local priest and I witnessed the extent to which he was prepared to serve others, particularly the poor and the weak. Somewhere in my mind I made the connection. I wanted to make a difference through a life of service as a priest. This led me to the seminary at Clonliffe College, Dublin. It was to be my first trip beyond Cork.

Simple events often have such far-reaching implications. I have just described one that impinged upon me as a strong impulse. It was to shape much of the rest of my life. I now see it as a divine appointment, as God's way of speaking to me in a way that I could understand at that time. It was an intervention of grace. There was to be another simple event that again would have a profound impact. I had been ordained about eighteen months. My first appointment included teaching in a vocational school and running a club for boys, most of whom were at risk. I had become very weary, which led to much dissatisfaction and analysis for me. I happened to pick up *Bury me in my Boots* by Sally Trench. She wrote about her work among the deprived and homeless in London. At times it over-taxed her. At one time as she lay in bed suffering from a nervous breakdown, she realised that her life had been spent in working for God. She now knew that her life was to be a working with God. Cold print on a page, but what an impact! The harvester has to wait for the rhythm of nature. I too need to work with the rhythm of God's plan for my life. I could clearly see that I had been making such a basic mistake.

I began to read every spiritual book I could find. Scripture was no longer a text book, but a living word. I began to speak, very tentatively at first, about my new found interest. When I was invited to my first prayer meeting, I stood somewhat confused at the spontaneity of praise and prayer. How people could get so much from a biblical reading intrigued me. I was somewhat ill at ease at the warmth with which people greeted one another. I had to go through much soul-searching, attempting to integrate what this seemed to be all about with what I already knew. I was not too sure that I would succeed. But something kept drawing me back. It all took up to eighteen months. I was prayed with on a number of occasions. There was no dramatic moment of conversion, but the gradual yielding to the Spirit of God and giving Him permission to work in His way in and through me. It was then too that I recognised that all I had been taught and knew intellectually was now taking on a new significance and importance for me. It was all part of who I was as a child of God. It was all part, too, of my richness as a child of a particular tradition.

Living the grace

I then became involved in leadership in the prayer meeting at Dublin Airport chapel. They were dramatic days, with more and more people attending, especially at the monthly healing Mass. I remember leading 120 people into a baptism of the Spirit, with the RTE cameras following me wherever I went. Then came my involvement in the International Charismatic Conference in 1978, which had an attendance of 30,000. More recently, I have acted as National Chaplain to the National Service Committee for Catholic Charismatic Renewal in Ireland.

I learned so much through all this time, sometimes at the cost of misunderstanding and weariness. I grasped a sense of God's sovereign reign. He is indeed Lord. Jesus became Healer for me. I witnessed this at first hand in my own life and in the lives of others. I now expect His healing touch to be manifest in the celebration of the sacraments, especially in the Eucharist and the Sacrament of the Sick and when we pray for the ill. He is Saviour, saving me from sin, fear, death and suffering. He desires to bring me into a relationship with the Father that is intimate and personal. I believe that His grace is sufficient for me. I know that a living faith, recognisable by the gift and fruit of the Spirit, is the norm for a person living a Christian life.

Brothers and sisters clarify the grace
I learned above all to appreciate the giftedness of the lay faithful. Ministry and God's gifts are not confined to a particular caste or set of people. His blessing and His grace are available to all who seek Him. So much of my testimony is a record of the times I have been encouraged and inspired in hearing the prayers of brothers and sisters in Christ with me and for me. So often I have heard from them a word of prophecy giving a renewed focus to my life. I grew more confident in the Lord and in myself in knowing of their affection and prayer for me. I learned so much about commitment in seeing their commitment to Christ and to His people. It has always inspired me when I see the input so many of them make in terms of energy, time and finance. I am particularly grateful to those who have journeyed with me in Charismatic Renewal and in a covenant community that I was part of at Bayside in Dublin.

The experience of cell groups
A further seemingly small and 'chance' event was again to give a new direction to my life. I had occasion to listen to a ten-minute input from Dom Pigi Perini, in San Eustorgio, Milan in May 1989. Through his broken English I understood that he spoke about the dramatic growth in his parish and the place of cell groups in the work of evangelisation there. I knew it was for me, even though I could barely hear what he said and certainly did not understand all he sought to communicate. A cell is a group of four to twelve people, committed to evangelisation and to multiplying itself. I know that it is because of the Lord's goodness that during the last seven years I, with parishioners in Ballinteer, in south Dublin, have been pioneering the cell system as a strategy of

parish evangelisation. At one time there were thirty-one cell groups in Ballinteer alone, with up to 300 engaged in the work of evangelisation. It has been adopted by at least ten parishes throughout Ireland. It has involved many invitations and much travel to speak at different locations.

In my understanding, to be Catholic is to be ecumenical. It is to know that Christ is a principle of unity. In Him we discover that together we belong to Him, that we are His body. A very happy chapter in my life was the partnership I formed with the Rev Peter Good of the Methodist community at Dundrum. We prayed, ate, laughed, planned, shared Scripture and also aspects of our work, together as equals. He often teased me that he was first with the cell group concept. His congregation had been founded by John Wesley based on small evangelistic units. Hence the name, as method or system of organisation. Peter's openness to God, his love for his people and his family and his evangelistic zeal were greatly inspirational for me. A genuine affection, respect and love developed between our two congregations, which was delightful to witness. This in turn led to many joint ventures.

It is all God's work

And what of now and the future? I don't know. I am deeply aware that God seeks our faithfulness amid the myriad of each day's unfolding. It is to attempt to bloom where we are planted, with His Spirit as our guide and wisdom. It is to tap into Him in the silence of our hearts, to hear Him in His Word, knowing that His transforming power is at work. It is to enter into daily worship with brothers and sisters. It is to embrace the crosses of each day and know that they too carry the seeds of resurrection and of new life. And perhaps there may be other small 'chance' events, which will point to new directions and horizons. Perhaps! I don't know. It will be His initiative. It is all God's work.

12

'SPUDS FOR THE PRODS'

REV NEAL CARLIN

*Neal was one of the first pioneers of renewal in the
Catholic Church in the early 1970s. He set up a
reconciliation ministry in Columba House in Derry
in what was a bombed out RUC station.*

I was born in Derry, in Ballyowen House, a large house
out in the country. My great-grandfather was a very rich
man, owner of many properties, including a wholesale
Wine & Spirit Merchants business in Derry's Waterside.
I have a relic of those days on the mantelpiece, an old
crockery bottle embossed with the words 'Neal Carlin &
Company 1840'. We found it, about three feet down,
when a digger was digging up the yard outside
the retreat centre established by Columba House
in Dundrean, Co. Donegal. My great-grandfather
employed a housekeeper from Donegal whose practice it
was to lace the children's milk with whiskey to put them
to sleep. This had a tragic outcome, in that both sons
became alcoholics at a very early age, one dying at the
age of eighteen and the other, my grandfather, dying at
the age of thirty-three.

We moved from Ballyowen House into the city, partly to escape from the constant, harassing visits to our
house by the RUC. That was back in 1940–42, during the
war. My father was known for his nationalist views, and
for being the sponsor of 'The Neal Carlin Cup' for Gaelic
football. He found himself the target of attention from

the police. My mother often talked of the RUC banging at the door at two or three o'clock in the morning, 'checking up on Republicans'. She would have to get up and make them tea. If they weren't given tea, they would return two or three times that week. If they were treated to the hospitality they demanded, they might not return until the following week. Nobody could do a thing about it. It was frustrating and demeaning for my father and others subjected to like treatment. Such behaviour formed part of the build-up to what was to erupt many years later in the rebellion following the civil rights campaign.

There were ten of us altogether in the family. We lived for a couple of years in Derry and then moved eleven miles away to Newtowncunningham, in the Republic of Ireland. It was a village associated with another village up the road, called Manorcunningham. Old man Cunningham had come across as one of the Planters from Scotland. They settled in what was the best land in this part of Donegal. There was a hot debate, around the time of partition, as to whether Donegal should be divided, with the eastern section being included in the new entity of Northern Ireland. All I recall is the great number of Presbyterian and Church of Ireland farmers – they owned all the land around that way. We had special school holidays for gathering the potatoes. We got three weeks off from our little three-room school every October, to gather spuds for the 'prods' (a shortened version of 'prodesans', as Protestants were colloquially called).

Anyway, I went to an all-Irish boarding college. All that was Gaelic was reinforced in me. For example, we were punished with a strap if we were caught playing soccer in the school grounds. I played Gaelic football for Donegal and did a lot of running. I got the surprise of my life in college when I won the mile race. I was sixteen and in my third year. In fourth and fifth year I won it again and then, all through the seminary, I won the cross-country and the mile. I love running. But today I'm 'coop-ered', as they say, with a sore foot, which is why I'm slimming these days. I need to lose weight.

It was 1958 when I left secondary school and entered the seminary. I had some difficult times there, finding it such a rigid system, with little room for compassion. I was ordained in 1964 and went to Scotland. I was still very involved with football and athletics. I was president of the Gaelic Athletic Association in Scotland for two years. I studied for a teaching qualification and began to teach religion in St Margaret's High School, Airdrie, in 1972. I was very friendly with ministers of different denominations. And then suddenly it happened – Bloody Sunday. Six of my brothers had been on the March on Bloody Sunday and they all gave me their reports. I felt helpless. Deep down memories of past injustices surfaced. I felt the Church was standing back and doing nothing. I felt passionately for my people at home, but didn't know what I could do to help. In those days, a lot of my friends were leaving the priesthood for various reasons and I began to agonise over whether I should stay or not. The upshot of all this turmoil was that I fell into a kind of a depression, which lasted for about six months.

Then I was moved to another parish. An old priest, John Cosgrove, rang me and asked if I would go to a prayer meeting in the house of a friend of his up in Stirling. As a courtesy to him I went. His friend, a recov-ering alcoholic, had a fourteen-year-old daughter who was suffering from leukaemia. There were just the four of us there: an old retired priest, a recovering alcoholic, a girl with leukaemia and a depressed curate. Quite a set-up! They passed round some song sheets and the three of them started singing. As they sang the song 'Spirit of the living God fall afresh on me', I began to get an inner peace. I found myself sitting there smiling. I was experi-encing the anointing and blessing of God. It was the beginning of something new.

An elder in the local Church of Scotland, gave me a book, *Nine o'clock in the Morning* by Dennis Bennett. I read there about forgiveness, about the reality of the power of Jesus Christ, about the Lord being alive in our hearts, about the power of the Spirit and His gifts that enable us to prophesy, to teach, to heal. I had heard about these things before, but here for the first time I was reading about somebody who had actually experienced the reality of them. I was very excited about that. It engendered in me a new hope. It was like coming alive again, being renewed in my spirit. I became more at peace with myself and with others. I told my Bishop that I now felt able to go back to work in Ireland.

I was given a temporary post in the Cathedral in Derry. For me now, the answer to the Troubles lay in the work of reconciliation, in preaching and teaching Christ as the only one who could overcome evil and violence. A prayer meeting was started in the Northlands Rehabilitation Centre for alcoholics and drug addicts. I was astounded at the power of God released in those gatherings. People were healed in mind and body. Miraculous things happened in abundance. We organised large conferences. Then, suddenly, I was asked to leave the Cathedral. To this day, I don't really know why. The Bishop in Scotland was very surprised and annoyed. He asked for an explanation, but wasn't given one.

That was a very painful time of rejection. I had considered myself married to the Church, but now felt betrayed. It actually became a physical pain in my stomach. In time, the Lord healed me, but it took a long time; for me, forgiveness came gradually, in layers. But God had a hand in it all – as Joseph said to his brothers, 'What you meant for evil, God meant for good.' Had I not been set aside in this way, Columba House for Prayer and Reconciliation would never have been established in Derry, nor would St Anthony's Retreat Centre in Dundrean, Donegal.

I got permission from my Bishop in Scotland to spend
six months in America – visiting various houses of
prayer. On arrival, the airport chaplain put me up for the
night. In my room there was a board with an inscription
on it that riveted my attention: 'They that wait on the
Lord shall renew their strength, they shall mount up
with wings as eagles; they will run and not grow weary,
walk and not faint'. It was Isaiah 40 verse 31. A short
time before, I had gone on retreat to Nunraw Abbey, a
Cistercian monastery in Scotland. While there, I had
received a clear impression of a large eagle in flight and
a strong sense that I was to wait on God. I had said to a
friend of mine, 'You know the Bible. Is there anything in
it about waiting and an eagle?' He couldn't find anything. Now here it was in front of my eyes. I remember
taking the piece of board outside and telling the first people I met how I had come 6,000 miles to get this text!

About a week later I was in San Diego and I went to
a large prayer meeting, of about 800 people. A man stood
up and said 'I have had a scripture given to me three
times this week, and I know it's for someone here.' I
instinctively knew that Isaiah 40 verse 31 was the scripture he was going to read. And he did. Some months
later, I was in a House of Prayer in New Jersey, with a Fr.
Brennan. I told him this story, and he threw open the
door of his room. There on the wall was a big painting of
an eagle with the text of Isaiah 40 verse 31 on it. He gave
it to me to bring home with me.

When I came back to Ireland, in October 1979,
Cardinal O'Fiach arranged for me to work as a kind of
freelance chaplain in the prisons. I had an appointment
with him one day to discuss my future and stopped in
Craigavon on my way to see him. I asked a man who was
out walking his dog if he knew where I could get a cup
of tea. And he said, 'You can come to my house, sir.' He
joked with me over tea about me, being a priest, having
tea in a Protestant house in a Loyalist area. There was a
book of Scripture readings lying on the table and I casu-

ally flicked it open. There facing me was Isaiah 40 verse 31. I sensed the Lord speaking to me very clearly, 'The cardinal is a good man, but I told you to wait on Me.' So when the cardinal offered me an appointment in his diocese, I said, 'If you don't mind, I really feel the need to wait and see what's going to happen.' And ultimately, after a long wait and much prayer, the answer came. I was sitting in Bethany House down in Wexford with Norman and Jean Ruddock, a Church of Ireland minister and his wife, and Fr. Staples, who had been my spiritual director in the seminary. After praying in tongues, there was a great silence, a great sense of God's presence. These words came clearly into my mind: 'In a few days you'll meet a stranger who'll point out to you a house.' That was exciting.

At that time, I was working one day a week in the Northlands Centre in Derry. That week, a man whom I'd never met before came up to me during coffee break and said, 'Father Neal, what you need is a large house. I know where you can get one.' He brought me down to Queen Street, to a bombed-out site, four storeys of rubble. And I knew, I just knew that that was it. I had £200 in my pocket, a broken-down old car and no income. I didn't know how it was going to come about, but I knew it was right. I woke up one morning with a person's name in my mind, a local builder. I went straight to him. He said, 'I don't have a lot of time, what is it?' I said, 'Two sentences. There's an old house in Queen Street. You buy it and I'll live in it.' He looked at me for about three seconds and said, 'OK.' It was as simple as that.

The building had almost been restored when the builder suddenly went bankrupt. He told me, 'I'm going to have to sell the house in a couple of weeks to somebody who'll give me a good price, unless you can come up with the money.' Then the pressure was on. We needed £30,000. The name came into my mind of someone I had met for about ten minutes at a retreat in Dublin. I somehow knew that if I drove to Dublin I'd see him at seven o'clock that night. So I went, and phoned for an appointment. His secretary said it was impossible, as he had a meeting scheduled with his accountant, who was flying in from London. I said, 'He'll meet me at seven o'clock tonight. I'm sure of it.' She rang at six and said, 'I don't know what has happened, but the meeting with the accountant has been cancelled. He wants you to come up here for dinner at seven.' I walked out of there two hours later with a plastic bag with £10,000 in it.

I thought to myself on the way home, 'I am either the greatest conman alive, or the Holy Spirit is at work!' And I knew the latter had to be true, because that guy was a shrewd businessman, yet he handed me ten thousand quid with no strings attached. The rest of the money came in just as dramatically. An old colleague of mine from Letterkenny, a retired psychiatrist, came to visit. One of the volunteer workers happened to mention to him that we were short of cash. My friend came to me and said, 'Would you be embarrassed if I gave you £20,000 free of interest for as long as you need it?' Apparently he had recently received precisely that sum, on his retirement. He had prayed about what to do with it, and felt the Lord wanted him to use it for some good purpose. So he put his retirement cheque in an envelope on top of his wardrobe and waited. And that is how the Lord provided for the building of what became Columba House, a centre for prayer and reconciliation. So I don't have to be told that the Lord is good and that He'll stick by you if you stick by Him.

Meanwhile I continued with my work in the prisons. We started two prayer and Bible study meetings in the H Blocks in Long Kesh, involving thirty to forty men. There was some concern among the Republican leadership when they learned that men were being converted to the Lord and turning away from Republicanism. I have letters from a lot of those men, saying how much they were blessed by those prayer meetings. Later, many of those prisoners were transferred to Magilligan Prison in Derry, where we attempted to start an interdenominational prayer meeting. I knew that some of the Catholic prisoners would have come to the prayer meeting but were not yet at the point where they could cross the Catholic/Protestant divide. I suggested that maybe we could facilitate these people and help further the reconciliation process by having two united prayer meetings per month and two meetings where Protestants and Catholics would meet separately. The next day, the Governor telephoned me and accused me of trying to undermine the integrationist policy of the prison. He told me I would no longer be allowed into the prison. When I tried to gain admittance, I discovered a red card in the pigeon hole allocated to me, barring me from all future admission.

Pressure had also been building from another Christian ministry at work in the prison, which seemed to have difficulties in really respecting the fact that Catholics could be Christians. The situation was compounded by the fact that a few of the Catholics who participated in the prayer meetings ended up being proselytised by members of fundamentalist, anti-Catholic denominations. I later learned that the Bishop held me responsible for this and told the prison chaplin not to invite me into the prison any more. I got the boot from both secular and Church authorities.

Looking back on that time of prison ministry, I can see how all the cracks in the Body were exposed and old fears, old prejudices, old hates, old long-standing notions of each other emerged. There has to be an immense conversion in the heart of Protestants in our country, a paradigm shift in the Protestant psyche, if they're going to love Catholics as Christians. And even more so, a Roman Catholic priest. I mean, whatever chance the ordinary Catholic has of being a Christian – how could a priest be a Christian? I praise God for those Protestant ministers who can openly embrace me as a brother. I sense the warmth of complete acceptance when it is there and am pained by the coldness of its absence. No amount of nice words and no amount of pleasantries can disguise the absence of brotherly recognition.

There is a non-residential community of fifty-eight full-time members attached to Columba House. We meet for prayer every Wednesday night and are committed to a range of caring activities in the local community. We are currently exploring, with the support of ministers from other denominations, the possibility of establishing a centre for the care of alcoholics and drug addicts. The centre would be located on a farm and I would see it very much as being a centre for spiritual renewal, with an integrated programme of prayer and physical work forming part of the healing process. I would greatly appreciate readers' prayers for the Lord's blessing and provision for this new project, the White Oaks Centre, Derryvane, Muff, Co. Donegal. It will be an interdenominational centre on the border between North and South, aiming to draw Christians together from different cultural and denominational backgrounds to join forces in caring for those suffering from the abuse of alcohol and drugs.

13

TEN YEARS IN JAIL FOR THE IRA

TOM KELLY

*Tom is a former IRA paramilitary who is now leader of a
men's Bible Study. He speaks regularly with a former
Loyalist paramilitary at meetings about how Jesus can
bridge the gap in Northern Ireland.*

I was born on July 23rd 1955 in Belfast. My parents had
a family of four; three boys and a girl. I am the second
eldest. For the first five years of my life we lived in the
Markets area, a small Catholic enclave situated at the
bottom of the Lower Ormeau Road. This area has experienced a lot of sectarian attacks and quite a lot of
oppression from Orange parades, which has now led to
open opposition from Catholics, protesting that they no
longer want to be treated to such dictatorial abuse. At
that time, our whole family lived with my grandmother.
It was a very small one-bedroom house and having
seven people living and sleeping together became a great
strain for my parents, particularly my mother.

Eventually my parents were allocated a new home, so
our family of six moved to a three-bedroom house in the
Turf Lodge area of West Belfast. At this time, 1960, Turf
Lodge could have been described as a new frontier. For
us kids it was nothing but green fields, running beauti-
fully along the bottom of the Black Mountain. To me it
was a paradise, a vastness to be explored and enjoyed
and that's what I did. I wasn't long in making friends
and it was, I suppose, a relief for my parents to see that

we were all happy in our new environment. Within my family, I was the most athletic. I spent most of my young life competing in sport, be it running or football. I played Gaelic football for my primary school and represented my secondary school, Christian Brothers, Glen Road, on the team which won the Belfast Inter Schools Cup. In all honesty, I enjoyed my school years. One year, I never missed a single day and had a letter of congratulation sent home to my mother.

Near the end of my school days, 'the Troubles' broke out in Northern Ireland. My parents knew what was going on, but we kids didn't have a clue. I remember seeing the ugly scenes on TV and I didn't like it. Nevertheless we all had to get on with our lives.

I left school at the age of fifteen and immediately began searching for work. It took me about three weeks before I got employment as a barman in the Balmoral Inn on the Lisburn Road, a predominantly Protestant area. I enjoyed working there and became quite liked by all the regular punters who came in on a daily basis. They knew I was a Catholic, as a lot of Catholics were in that employment. I had my first political argument there, with two girls on the kitchen staff. They were Protestants and had been bragging about how good it was that British soliders were now positioned in Catholic areas. I said to them, 'How would you like it if you woke up some morning and found Irish soldiers all over the place?' They didn't take it too well and reported me to the boss. I had to apologise.

As the Troubles progressed, the IRA became more daring in their activities. I noticed anger and hostility raising its head amongst the punters. Then one night the IRA exploded a bomb in White's Bakery a few doors down from the pub, which helped bring my job to an end. People were crying out for a backlash and that, to my young mind, spelt danger. I no longer felt safe, so I left.

Unfortunately, after that I found it entirely impossi-

ble to find work closer to home, as Catholic areas were
greatly under-privileged, so I had to sign on the dole.
Most of my friends were unemployed, so we all began to
hang around street corners. We all noticed the IRA activity within the area. We watched barricades going up and
joined in the odd riot or two. The whole area had a siege
mentality and people spoke of nothing else but the IRA.
My dad began to tell me stories about the old IRA and
how he once was connected but left because a priest
warned him about his soul. He told me he didn't want to
hear Jesus say to him, 'Depart from me ye cursed'. Those
words scared me at the time, but being young, I soon put
them behind me. My dad was a very good churchgoer,
but suffered badly from a nervous condition. He was in
and out of a psychiatric hospital. He began to stay
indoors for longer periods, and eventually took to bed,
leaving my mother the burden of raising us kids, a real
handful.

I became more daring. I began to stay out longer and
began to mix more with the kind of people that
inevitably drew the attention of the IRA. Some of my
mates belonged to active Republican families, so they
were able to vouch for me and I joined Fianna Eireann,
still at the age of fifteen. I learned how to break down a
weapon, clean it and put it back together again. Because
I was tall, full of confidence and really eager, the IRA
took me into their ranks, even though I was still so
young.

Almost immediately after I joined, I engaged the
British Army on the Monaghan Road. I fired my first
shot! The adrenalin raced through me; it was the first
time ever that I experienced absolute power – power
over life or death and – I chose death. I became con-
sumed by the concept of violence, scheming every day,
looking for my prey – be it soldiers or police. I didn't
care; I had to satisfy this rage within me. My comrades
began to see a psycho on the loose. I feared nothing nor
any situation. I was always first in the line of active duty.

I didn't care for my safety, nor did I think about my family and so I became more and more detached from them and more and more deeply empowered by active violence.

One day, while I was on active service, word reached me that my father had passed away. It was February 26th 1972. I had spoken to him just that morning. I had found it odd that he should ask me to look after my mum and not to bring her any trouble. He had been in bed for days. I remember running down through the streets of Turf Lodge and bursting through my mother's front door, to find the neighbours and a priest praying the rosary. I ran up the stairs, to find my mum talking to the doctor about my father's medication. He had taken a massive overdose. We buried and mourned him, but I couldn't make my mind up whether I loved his memory or hated it. Here I was, sixteen years old, wanting to change the world and people's thinking by the use of a gun, and I didn't realise that I had become a very bitter individual.

I carried on with my activities, regardless of my comrades telling me to take time off and, because of it, in February 1973, I was finally arrested and interned in Long Kesh for two and a half years. My experience in Long Kesh was mixed. I made some good friends and we all bonded well together. We dug many tunnels. One man called Hugh Cooney was shot dead escaping from one. That was after we burnt nearly the entire camp!

Every five weeks or so, the Governor called in British Army soldiers to raid the cages (the wire-meshed enclosures in which we were imprisoned) looking for 'Republican paraphernalia', or any signs of escape tunnels. They would burst in an hour or so before dawn. They would shout at us to stand by our beds with knife, cup, fork and spoon, and any valuables we had. Each item of clothing was searched before we were allowed to put it on. Then we were ordered to run a gauntlet of two lines of baton-wielding soldiers and dogs which stretched from the door of the hut to another building, usually the canteen. If we didn't run fast enough, the batons and dogs helped us on our way. The soldiers turned the huts inside out, and when they were finished, we had to run the gauntlet back again. This unpublicised form of British justice stoked up the fires of burning resentment.

When I was freed in 1975, I was a very angry person indeed and I couldn't wait to settle some scores. I didn't have to wait long before I got the calling card again and so resumed IRA activities.

I was now twenty years old and I was full of hatred and resentment and was being used to full potential. I was again going down the road of no return. I was on a self-destruct journey of retaliation, so that eventually, once again, I found myself arrested, in August 1976, and charged with attempted murder of a British soldier, possession of a weapon with intent and IRA membership.

I was brought to Crumlin Road Jail in Belfast where a whole new nightmare was to unveil itself to me. Paramilitaries were no longer given political status. We were all to be criminalised and were being forced by the prison regime to live together. That is, Republicans were expected to socialise with Loyalists – sworn enemies. We found ourselves fighting every day, shouting abuse out through our cell doors. It got so bad that we had to be locked up twenty-four hours a day. I lost a lot of remission. None of us wanted to conform. News came to me one day that my attempted murder charge was dropped because of some legality, so, in the year of 1977, I was sentenced to seven years for the possession charge and began my time in the H-Blocks.

I was brought to H-Block 5. When I arrived, two prison warders asked me if I was in the IRA. I said, 'Yes'. They replied, 'At least you're honest,' and didn't touch me. Quite a lot of beatings were being reported then. I refused to conform by wearing a prison uniform or doing work, so I was locked up for five and a half years, twenty-four hours a day, in solitary confinement. We began the 'Dirty Protest' and were known as the 'Blanket Men'.

All any man had in their cell was a Bible. I used the pages in it, after I had read it, for making cigarettes. I called it having a holy smoke. Most of the lads would say the rosary every night, reciting it out through their cell doors in Irish. Since we had no writing materials, I used to use the crucifix in my cell to write on the white painted walls. It left a mark like a pencil. We were all learning how to speak Irish, and that was the only way we had of writing down the vocabulary. As the protest progressed, the situation became more desperate. We had two hunger strikes. Ten men died, most of them friends of mine, especially Kieran Doherty, who had played on the same school team as me.

My release from this hell was in February 1982. A day I won't forget. I felt small, isolated, afraid and unhappy. I couldn't adjust to life for some time. All my surroundings had changed so much and, although there was a banner hanging across the front of my mother's home saying, 'Welcome Home Tom', I didn't feel that I was home. I felt empty. I felt that life was worthless. I began to ask myself, where had my life gone? What had I achieved? The answer was, nothing! I saw only death, hatred and ruination. I didn't want this, so I decided that I wouldn't get involved in violence anymore. I was now twenty-seven years old.

After a few days hanging around the house and doing nothing, an old friend called to see me. We took a walk down to Milltown Cemetery. We looked at all the graves. I remember feeling as dead as they were, so it was then that I gave myself a kick. I started to go out again and I began frequenting the Social Club in Turf Lodge.

I got a job behind the bar of a Social Club on the Glen Road. It was there that I met my future wife, Catherine. We got married and had five girls; I saw each of them being born! Their births truly opened my eyes to the importance of the sacredness of life. Although I wasn't involved in violence any more, the Social Club in Turf Lodge became my local stop and, as it was a Republican Club, the IRA made me secretary of it for about three years. It was a job in which I felt I was being handled like a puppet. There was always some lackey of the IRA lurking in the background, checking that things went their way.

Meantime, my wife was more in need of me than the club was. She was going on religious pilgrimages and one day she asked me to go with her on one. So I went to Mt Melleray with her. There were a lot of people going. I must have gone about four times before I asked myself what I was doing, but, on this particular occasion I remember looking closely at all the people. They were praying, hugging each other, laughing and talking lovingly about God. I asked myself what it was that they had that I hadn't. What was the big difference between them and me? Within minutes the answer hit me.

I felt God saying to my mind, 'Tom, I want your heart' and, after a little time of thought, I remember responding by saying, 'If You want my heart, then take it. Take its hardness, its blackness and use it.' This happened in 1986. From that day, I haven't had one regret. Each day, life holds excitement in it. Not long after, in that same year, God brought into my life an American priest called Fr. Ed Wade, who, at the time, was like a new father to me.

He himself was an ex-American marine, trained to kill or maim, but God took him clean away from it and made him a man of God. A man with God's Spirit oozing out of him. He taught me things about God that I had never realised. He had me baptised in the Spirit. He opened my mind to new ways of thinking so that my old ways of thinking were completely obliterated. He brought me out of my wee box and had me see how other Christians praised and worshipped God. I felt the love for God in these people and, above all, for me. My

mind was about to explode. This was a revelation to me,
love God, **love** neighbour. I had to first learn to **love**
myself.

I was afraid to show love. I believed no one was low
enough to deserve the shallow love that was beginning
to burn inside me. So, I was asking God to do more with
me. In fact, work a miracle. Then, one Sunday evening,
Fr. Ed Wade telephoned me and asked me to come up to
Poleglass, where he said he was doing something with a
gathering of men. I went up to the Parish Priest's house,
called Cloona, and when I walked in there were over
forty men seated. I didn't know any of them. I felt very
uncomfortable. Fr. Ed Wade began praising God. We
sang songs, then he spoke of God's love, God's power,
God's sovereignty. He pulled no punches. It was man to
man stuff, no wimps allowed: and then it happened. He
asked me to witness and I found myself talking to forty
men. I began to let go of my pain. I repented before them
and God and I was received by all with nothing but love
and compassion. We've been meeting every Monday
night since then to this present day. The love that I have
experienced from these men you cannot buy. We've
accepted our Christian manhood and our Christian
brotherhood, with all the resulting joy and responsibili-
ties, and with Christ as our leader.

We try to live the gospel, both spiritually and practically, as best we can. We call ourselves 'The Light of
Christ Men's Group' – a name that came to us from Luke
8 verse 16, after three years of asking. Jesus was
described as the light of the world, so then, if we
Christians are to follow Him, we must extend that light
for Him. We cannot do this with any kind of prejudice or
malice in our hearts. I thank God that he has taken all the
bitterness and resentment from me. I can look at British
soldiers now with no trace of hatred. I see them as just
ordinary human beings like myself.

I prayed to God for a purpose, since my life had been
a mess. My only question was what good could I do

now? The Lord really is champion. He astounds me every time. I was introduced to the Maranatha Community, an interdenominational group, whose only concern is to bring God's healing, through repentance, to all communities. I shared one night at a meeting in Poleglass and a beautiful lady called Pauline approached me. She said that she would like me to meet her husband Jim, that he was once like me. I met Jim in Cookstown Town Hall. We talked. Jim was interned, like myself, and was in the UVF, a Protestant paramilitary group. Both Jim and myself repented to one another, hugged one another and became great friends. We repented before God and all the people present. After that we found ourselves invited to the House of Lords in Westminster, sharing with the cream of British politics. The Lord healed many troubled minds that day.

Jim is now one of the leaders of the Light of Christ Men's group. The group is open to Christians from every denomination. Protestant folk from East Belfast and other areas of the city have come to our Monday night meetings. We invite speakers from different churches to come and teach the Scriptures. Alcoholics, drug addicts, child molesters – all have found a welcome and the chance to learn that life is worth living, that God is a loving God who can be trusted, a God who can change lives. We have had the wonderful privilege of seeing God at work in the lives of hundreds of men over the years since the group started.

God has led us in different ways of service and growth. We have made a documentary for Dutch Television. We are now in the process of setting up small cell groups for those wanting more committed disciple-ship and fellowship. We, as a group, have visited many places of worship. We have been, for example, to Orangefield Presbyterian Church, where we shared our love for God and one another. They, in return, visited us in Poleglass. We praise the same God. We pray to the same God and live by the same commands of the same God.

You see, fundamentally, God wants people to live by the law of showing and giving love. If you who read this have no love for a particular person or, more generally, for your neighbour, whatever they may be, then you are captive to the strategy that Satan is employing in his drive to destroy Christendom. He candy-coats us all and we're rotten inside. I thank God for taking me through my hell, but more for what I can do to repair some of the damage. God wants to use us all, but we must have a heart fit for Him. We have to have a heart big enough for all humanity; after all, God's bigger than humanity. We must trust in God's providence.

Our inheritance is not of this world but the next, and I feel it's time that all the churches took the lead and, instead of peeping over the sides of our appointed boxes, it's time we came out of them and were seen. I had to travel a bitter road before I discovered that the real prison for me was not Long Kesh Internment Camp, but my own heart, which was captive to all manner of prejudice, fear, hatred, resentment and unforgiveness. We all need, in some way, to ask God to lead us out of our heart-prisons. Let us taste the love of neighbour, so that the shining light of Jesus Christ will blind the eyes of the deceiver. May God bless the minds and hearts of all who read this.

Jesus is Lord.

14

THAT WE MAY BE ONE

VERONICA FLYNN

Veronica is a home maker. Involved in the Evangelical Catholic Initiative, she co-ordinates various North/South projects and is involved in prayer ministry and in her local parish prayer group.

As I write this account of my walk with God, I am looking out over the trees in our garden to Killiney Hill, which is only a couple of miles from where I was born in South County Dublin. The course my life has taken so far is not at all unusual. I have always lived in suburbia and done suburban things. I was educated in a convent school, spent a year away in Spain, and worked at various jobs, none of which was in any way fulfilling. No Damascus Road encounter for me, but rather a trudge along the road to Emmaus, without ever having heard of the place, much less being aware of its relevance in my life.

From early childhood, I was always aware of God, my Father. I talked to Him all the time. I brought everything to Him. When I was lonely or depressed, He was the One I cried out to. When circumstances were difficult I would ask Him to help me cope. I did not have a close relationship with family or friends, so I became very self-sufficient and independent, but was always aware of the presence of God.

I was brought up in the Roman Catholic Church and observed its commands and traditions, which I saw as a means of pleasing God and getting closer to Him. As I have said, I was rather a loner and extremely shy, especially with men. As a result, my teenage years were unhappy ones. I never believed I would have a loving relationship or get married, as I had real difficulty in sharing my feelings with anyone! But nothing is impossible with God! I met Dermod and our love overcame my fear of commitment. We were married thirty years ago this year! I had never imagined such happiness. My life was transformed. In due course we had three girls. Dermod's career floundered a bit and we struggled with financial difficulties, but we remained very committed to one another and supported one another all the way.

During this time I began to feel there must be more to knowing God than I was experiencing, but no group I joined seemed to provide what I was looking for. I was still a practising Catholic, but was interested in other spiritual disciplines, including Yoga, TM, etc. Thank God, I never committed myself to any of these. At this time, I discovered I was expecting our fourth child. Our three other girls were thirteen, twelve and eight years old. I found my unexpected pregnancy very upsetting because, after the other children were born, I had really struggled with anxiety and depression and with just not being able to cope. As I saw myself as being self-sufficient and very capable, this was difficult to accept and I blamed my inability to cope on some nebulous physical disorder. So here I was, forty and expecting a baby and depressed at the thought of what lay ahead. Friends tried to reassure me, but to no avail. In desperation I read a self-help book on how to overcome difficulties, not realising it was a Christian book; it kept referring to the Lord Jesus as the One who helps. I was tempted to stop reading, as I didn't like that kind of talk. Too religious! However, I persevered. There were many pieces of Scripture quoted in that book about Jesus being the source of help, forgiveness and love and these found a response in my heart. During the first months of our new daughter's life I depended on those scriptures whenever I became anxious. During the night feeds, I would repeat them and I was not only encouraged by them, but my heart was being prepared to accept Jesus as my Lord and Master. I was not depressed or fearful and our new baby, now sixteen years old, was such a joy and blessing and brought great happiness to us all. She still does!

A few months later, to keep a friend company, I went to my first charismatic prayer meeting – Mount Zion Prayer Group. I had been warned to expect the unusual and I did find it strange, but the response in my heart to the worship of God felt so right; it was like coming home. I didn't understand it, but I knew this was what I had been searching for. There was no quick surrender. There were too many defences around my heart and the Lord's dealings with me have always been gradual. But as I was coming before Jesus more and more, praising His Name, reading and listening to His Word, so I let Him get closer to me. Meeting Him in His Word has been such a blessing to me and He continues to reveal Himself as I continue my journey with Him. This journey involves spreading the Good News among fellow Catholics, working for reconciliation among Christians and encouraging an awareness of our Jewish roots and our common destiny.

I belong to ECI (Evangelical Catholic Initiative), which is comprised of Catholic Christians who work for a Christ-centred, biblically-based renewal in the Catholic Church. To this end, we have organised conferences where the emphasis has been on the Good News of salvation and the importance of the Word of God in our lives. At these conferences, we always include speakers from other Christian denominations, who share their gifts and insights with us and through whom we have all been mightily blessed. As a result, relationships have been built up which have enabled us to engage in joint undertakings between the different Churches and on both sides of the border. I believe unity among

Christians is so close to the heart of Jesus that, as we draw closer to Him, we draw closer to other Christians, and so help to bring about His Kingdom here on earth. Through my relationships with Christians of other denominations, I have been involved in various cross-community ventures and have been so aware of the blessing there is where brothers and sisters in Jesus Christ meet and work together in His Name. Psalm 133 says, 'How good and pleasant it is when brothers live together in unity.'

The latest project we are jointly involved with is the United Prayer Initiative in which we are inviting Christians from the North and the South to commit to pray for one hour per week for a period of two years for the island of Ireland. The focus of the prayer is threefold:

(1) that God will bring about a spiritual revival in Ireland;
(2) that our sectarian attitudes would be changed;
(3) that a fair and just political settlement be implemented in Northern Ireland.

This Initiative has the support and involvement of believers from all the Christian denominations, North and South. We want to mobilise Christians all over the land to seek the Lord and pray for their country.

Since coming to know Jesus, I have joined a women's prayer movement called Lydia Prayer Fellowship, which involves the commitment to meet with other Lydia members, at least once a month, preferably once a week, to come before the Lord and seek what is on His heart for prayer, whether it be for His Church, for various problems in the country or for His people, Israel. We have been blessed to see many answers to prayer. The Lord is just waiting for us to come before Him with confidence, seeking His face, turning from our own ways and He will answer.

To know Jesus, it is necessary to read His Word, and

the promoting of Bible study is another area I have been drawn into, particularly the Alpha course, which is a wonderful explanation of the Christian faith. It is a biblically-based method of drawing people into a closer relationship with Jesus and, at the same time, because it is so important for believers to grow in their faith through a knowledge of the Word of God, it encourages people to read Scripture and experience for themselves the teachings of Jesus. We would dearly love to see this Alpha course being given in parishes all over the country, perhaps as a follow-on to Life in the Spirit seminars. To this end we arrange seminars which will encourage leaders in parishes and faith communities to undertake these courses.

Looking back on my journey through life, I thank God for keeping me in His Name and for the many blessings I have received. As I continue my walk with Jesus at my side, sharing what I have received with others on the way, I am mindful of Paul's words in 1 Corinthians 13:12:

Now we see but a poor reflection as in a mirror, then we shall see face to face. Now I know in part, then I shall know fully, even as I am fully known.

To God be the glory!

15

THE GRACE TO FORGIVE

HARRY MCCANN

Harry McCann is a lay Catholic leader in County Antrim.
He had both legs blown off in a major bomb explosion.
He is the leader of a local prayer group.

Twenty years ago I had a serious 'accident'. Someone
planted a bomb below my car, outside my jeweller's
shop in Antrim, my home town. Whether it was a
Loyalist or Republican attack was never discovered. No
group ever acknowledged responsibility. As I started the
car, the bomb exploded. I lost both my legs and suffered
severe abdominal injuries. Both my eardrums were
perforated and my face and hands were lacerated.

I have two indelible memories of that day. One is of
recovering consciousness momentarily before the ambulance arrived and looking up into the face of a neighbour,
Francis Cooney, and finding myself saying 'May God
forgive the people who did this to me'. The other is of
coming to again as I was being rushed to hospital in the
ambulance and hearing, in a faraway, almost objective
kind of way, these words coming from my lips again and
again: 'Father, forgive them for they know not what they
do.'

That could only have been the grace of God at work
in me. It had to be an on-the-spot, God-given grace, for I
had not previously been a forgiving kind of person at all.
But now I had no feelings of anger, hatred or revenge,
nor did I, through all the tortuously slow and painful

process of physical healing and rehabilitation that followed. Whoever planted that bomb fully intended to cause maximum damage, and death if possible. Yet I had only forgiveness in my heart towards them. Only the merciful grace of God Almighty could account for that.

In those early days, following my release from intensive care, a steady stream of visitors from Antrim, and further afield, came to sit by my hospital bed and express their sorrow and sympathy over what had happened. Many of these were Protestants. As they spoke of their revulsion and anger against those who had planted the bomb, my response was always the same: 'Yes, it was a terrible and pointless deed. But I have forgiven them, and I hope God has forgiven them.'

I had letters of sympathy and support from the ministers of all the Protestant churches in Antrim, and public prayers were offered for my recovery in all their services. In the hospital, the staff, Protestant and Catholic, gave of their very best to me – without the slightest regard for religious or political affiliation. All of this meant a great deal to me. Even to this day, Protestant acquaintances from that period in my life occasionally approach me in the street and express their regret for what happened to me, apologising for not having had the opportunity to visit me at the time. Their astonishment at my expression of forgiveness for the bombers serves to remind me of the sheer magnitude and effective reality of the grace of God.

Such acts of violence have sadly not been uncommon in Northern Ireland, dramatically changing the lives of many, many people. The damage caused has often gone beyond what is physical, causing people who have been hurt so terribly to become eaten up with thoughts of revenge. But, against all the odds, others have somehow grown closer to God as a result of what has happened to them, and have found the grace to forgive. This has been true for me. I have become so much more aware of God's goodness and mercy and know that it is from Him that I have received the grace of forgiveness. Without Him, I could not have borne what happened to me.

After long months of physiotherapy, I eventually managed to master the art of walking on two artificial legs. In time, I learned to drive a specially adapted car. With my new found mobility, I was able, in a small way, to demonstrate my gratitude for the kindness and concern shown me by so many Protestant people. I volunteered to chauffeur elderly folk from the local Nursing Home to their various churches on Sundays – Presbyterian, Methodist, Church of Ireland – wherever they wished to go.

One day, I heard that Prison Fellowship was asking for car owners to volunteer, at their own expense, to drive family members, who could not afford to pay for transport, to visit their relatives in Magilligan Prison. This prison housed convicted paramilitaries. It was an hour's drive away, and detours had to be made to pick up people at different points along the way. A friend of mine was aghast when he learned that I had volunteered my services. 'Don't you know,' he exploded, 'that you may very well be transporting family members of the very people who planted the bomb under your car?' In fact, on one occasion when I called at a house to pick up a lady, she refused to get into the car when she discovered who was driving. One of my other passengers explained to me that, following the blowing up of my car, this lady's husband had been arrested, and she was afraid I might 'say something to her' about it. In spite of assurances to the contrary, she declined my offer of a lift. It really made no difference to me whether or not I was helping the families of those who had caused my injuries. God had enabled me to truly forgive, without any residue of resentment.

Over the years I have had the privilege of testifying to the living reality of Jesus Christ and the effectiveness of His grace in my life in many different church settings – from little non-denominational house meetings in the

Antrim hills to the Church of Ireland's St Anne's Cathedral in Belfast. I have spoken in the Pentecostal church in Darkley, which witnessed the cold-blooded murder of worshippers at the hands of Republican gunmen. I have testified to the power of Christ alongside fellow Christians such as Noreen Hill, whose husband, a grammar school headmaster, still exists in a comatose state so many years after being struck down in the Remembrance Day bombing in Enniskillen, and Michael McGoldrick, whose son was murdered by Loyalist gunmen in Lurgan during the Drumcree disturbances two years ago. I have sat in sympathy with the family of the young policeman who murdered several people in the Sinn Fein offices in Belfast and then shot himself. I have travelled to many parts of Ireland, and still do when asked, on reconciliation missions with teams from the Christian Renewal Centre in Rostrevor. Always the message is the same, the simple yet powerful truth that there is forgiveness to be found in Jesus Christ. As I make my way to the front and stand somewhat awkwardly before people on two artificial legs, I find that I don't need many words to convey what great things God has done in my life, how wonderful it is to know Him.

Sometimes it seems to take a trauma in our lives to bring us close to the Lord. My 'trauma' came with a bang. Before that, I'm ashamed to admit, though I thought I was a good Catholic, I had been merely going through the motions, mechanically performing what I considered to be the duties required of me. I did not realise that mere practices cannot make anyone a Christian.

I now realise that without my Saviour, Jesus Christ, I would be totally lost. He brought me through my accident twenty years ago. His greatness and mercy is not something I've read about in the lives of other people. I have experienced the reality of it in my own life. I have a living awareness of God's presence within me and know His willingness to share all my ups and downs, to help

me in my times of need and distress. I have grown in the
knowledge of Him by regularly reading the Bible, and
find that He enables me to live in accordance with His
teachings, however difficult I sometimes find that to do.

I am sometimes saddened by the reproach of other
Christians, who question my sincerity, asking me how I
can say I am a Christian and yet remain in the Catholic
Church. They seem to think it's impossible for a Catholic
to get to heaven without renouncing his Catholic faith.
The Catholic Church, they say, is not a Christian Church
at all. Yet it has been my experience that, as I have grown
in an understanding of the faith handed down to me in
the Church into which I was born, I have come to a
deeper appreciation of the vastness of the loving kindness of God, of His personal care and concern for all who
are in pain or sorrow. Participating in the Eucharist came
to mean so much more to me, after my experience of
twenty years ago. The Scripture readings at Mass came
alive to me as never before, and I enjoyed a sense of the
nearness of the presence of God which I found, and still
find, nowhere else. Our tradition is not perfect – which
part of the divided Body of Christ is? Yet I am glad to be
where I am, because this is where I experience the living
presence of Jesus Christ with me. He loves this part of
His Body, as He does all the other parts. He does not
despise or reject us. There is a great depth of riches of the
knowledge of God, of His Son Jesus Christ and of His
Holy Spirit in the Catholic Church. Is it not time for all of
us who truly follow Christ to look rather for the treasure
that God has been able to preserve in the different parts
of His Church, than to look for what we can condemn?

I believe that now is the time for all of us who profess
to be Christian to put behind us the wrongs of the past,
whether we have been the injured ones, or have ourselves caused injury in any way. We need to turn to the
Lord God and ask for His forgiveness and mercy, and
seek to make amends, in so far as possible, for the
wrongs of the past. There is no other way to real peace in

this country of ours.

I thank the Lord for bringing me thus far. My prayer is that what I have shared here will help in some way to bring new light to some who are still without the knowledge of His presence in their lives.

16

I AM AN ALCOHOLIC

MARTIN KELLY

Martin is a Youth Leader and a garage manager, with a strong testimony of deliverance from alcohol, suicide and depression. Martin also leads a youth prayer group.

My name is Martin. I am an alcoholic. Born and reared in Dublin, I am the youngest of ten children. I don't remember too much about my early years. I remember being very attached to my mother, a very prayerful woman. She used to take me with her to work – cleaning other people's houses. I could never understand why she had to do that kind of work – wash and iron their clothes, scrub their floors, clean their toilets. I always felt that she was so much greater than the people she worked for.

My father was a merchant seaman, so we saw little of him. He had a drink problem. I had a great fear of him, especially when he was drinking whiskey, because he would become violent. I remember one night there was a particularly violent row. There was blood all over the furniture and the walls. I lay petrified, listening to the commotion and when it finally ended and Dad fell asleep downstairs, I crept into my mother's bed. I promised her that when I grew up I would make up to her for all the unhappiness and heartache she had to suffer because of her family. I would give her the life she deserved. I would look after her and care for her the rest of her life. 'Go back to bed, son,' she whispered. 'Don't worry about me. I'll be all right.'

I was so fearful of my father that I found great difficulty talking to him. Having a normal conversation with him was very hard work for me. One day, while Dad was away at sea, the gas company man called to cut off the supply because my mother had been unable to pay the bill. She was quite distressed because the gas provided light and cooking for herself and her ten children.

Attempted suicide

Later that night I was awakened by a commotion out on the landing. Peeping out, I saw that my brother and sister were holding on to my mother and marching her to and fro. Then they took her into the bathroom, where my brother tried to make her sick by putting his fingers down her throat. Later I learned that she had become so distraught over her predicament – unable to pay bills or buy essentials and having to deal with all the problems on her own – that she had taken an overdose of sleeping pills. She was seriously ill and was taken into St Brendan's psychiatric hospital, while we children were taken into various Charitable Homes around Dublin. I bitterly hated those places, because of the unchristian treatment I experienced in them.

One of my most distressing memories of my beloved mother was when my father took me from the Home to see her in hospital. She was not in her bed and we were asked to wait in the ward and told that she would be back shortly. After about five minutes some hospital staff carried her into the ward on a stretcher. Her face was wild and distorted with pain and she was shaking from head to toe. There was a kind of stick in her mouth. I learned later that she had been for electric shock treatment and the thing in her mouth was to prevent her biting her tongue.

I remember thinking, 'If only they would listen to what you have to say they would realise that it isn't shock treatment you need – you simply need money to pay your bills and support your children.' The memory

reminds me of Mary when they were crucifying Jesus.
She must have had similar thoughts: 'If only they would
listen to you. If only they could realise what you are
offering them.'

I wanted to appeal to my father but he had always
taught us that we must not speak out of turn. We had to
respect our elders and to hold our tongue unless we
were spoken to. I was to see my mother in distress and
pain many more times.

New beginning – false start
The time came when I thought I had seen the end of all
that confusion and fear. My mother came out of hospital
and we moved from our two-bedroom house to a three-
bedroom house in a different area. But our ordeal had
not ended. The local residents got up a petition against
us. They didn't want such a large family moving into
their neighbourhood. Furthermore, they were house
owners, while we were only renting the house. I remember well the coldness of those people and my mother's
distress. Indeed it was not too long until she had another breakdown. She was taken into hospital and we were
sent back to those dreadful Homes once again.

I think it must have been then that I began to ask
whether there was a God at all. Where was this all-pow-
erful, all-loving, merciful Father that Jesus spoke about
now? Was He asleep, or deaf or dead? Did He exist at
all? That night I prayed half-heartedly in my bed, just
staring up at the ceiling. All the time the thought kept
breaking through that there was no God; because the
God I had been brought up to revere and trust could not
abandon His children and be deaf to their cries of distress.

Still no respite
Time passed and our term in the Home came to an end.
We returned to what was a mere semblance of home. My
brothers had become young men, aimless, shiftless, bel-

ligerent. They were the inevitable product of their brutish life. Their refuge from the harshness of their situation was in alcohol. They got drunk with increasing frequency; and when they were drunk they vented their anger and frustration on each another and on whoever happened to be within easy reach.

A voice crying in the wilderness

The turning point in my life came when I felt I had hit rock bottom. It was the time I finished up in Mountjoy Jail after a night out of my mind on drugs and drink. Suddenly I was on my knees, praying desperately. 'Lord get me out of here and I'll do anything you want me to do. I'll become a priest or a monk.' I had often made those kinds of promises to God when there was no other way to go. Always I forgot the promises when the crises had passed. It was as though God was reminding me of my infidelity.

Later that evening, in my cell, I suddenly heard a voice shouting something outside. I was vividly reminded of the text about John the Baptist: '. . . a voice crying in the wilderness, "Prepare the way for the Lord." ' I realised vaguely that Jesus, during all those terrible years of my life, had somehow gone before me to prepare the way, to lead me out of the darkness into the light. Phase one of this deliverance was, alas, to be marred by my fickleness of heart. Getting out on bail the following Tuesday, I went to the nearest pub to celebrate – by getting drunk!

Mother's terrible secret

One evening my mother began to behave in a bizarre way and I knew she was heading for another breakdown. When I arrived home, I found the living room full of statues and religious pictures. They were on the telly, on the mantlepiece, on the table. I was seized with a sudden hatred of God once more. This poor woman, who had suffered so much and had prayed so faithfully and fervently, had been, apparently, abandoned by God. Here she was about to be committed again, to face the pain and loneliness of the mental hospital. In my rage I set about smashing all the statues and pictures and tearing them to shreds.

Later that night my mother let me in on a terrible secret. When she was a child, she had been sexually abused. When she was a teenager, she had been raped by her uncle. As if that had not been burden enough, she told me, my father had been having affairs with other women – some even in our own street. No wonder the poor soul was being so tormented in her mind!

When she was sent off to St Patrick's Hospital, I went to see her. I got a basin of water and washed her feet. In the middle of that I began to weep openly. 'Ma,' I said, 'when you die you'll go straight to heaven. Jesus is going to make you a great saint. When you die, go to Jesus and ask him to forgive all my sins. And ask him, when he takes you, to take me too because I just couldn't live without you.'

For the umpteenth time they pumped drugs into my mother to remove her from the pain of reality. It broke my heart to see the effect the treatment was having on her. Once I saw her crawling around on the floor, under the beds. She had taken to tearing the wallpaper and taking other patients' property and stowing it away. It broke my heart to see her in such a lamentable state. My brother Tom, noticing my distress at the sight of her, came over to me and said: 'Martin, our mother is a very sick woman and they are doing whatever can be done for her, but you are even sicker. When are you going to do something to help yourself?'

Seizing this opening, I unburdened myself of much of what lay heavily upon my mind, weighing down my spirit, destroying my body and mind. I told him about my five-year-old affair with a married woman. 'There's no sense in trying to change,' I sobbed, 'because I'm already doomed to hell.' But Tom brushed aside all my

fears and told me about AA and their dependence on a
'Power Higher than Yourself'.

That very evening, I went to my first AA meeting. It
was the beginning of fresh hope, of a new optimism.
It was the first step on the long road back. There was no
overnight transformation, however – no Damascus Road
conversion. I was having a terrible struggle against the
drink. I was still dealing in stolen property. I was driving
a car around with no tax or insurance. My heart was still
a heart of stone.

Mother's sudden death

Some months later, mother died suddenly. Her death
dealt a shattering blow to all the ambitious plans I had
for her life. I renewed my determination to keep that
promise I had made to her years before. Her funeral
Mass was the first Mass I had attended in nine years. I
received Communion with great gratitude and a deep
sense of reverence. While I was still sitting there in the
company of the Lord, a little nun came over to me and,
taking my hand, she gave me a word of real encouragement.

That was another turning point for me. I began to count
my blessings. In spite of the things that had been wrong
in my life, I had been off the drink for nearly a year. I
began to build on that victory and two months later I had
more blessings to count: I had my health, I had my own
business. Yet, these victories were all of a material kind.
Within me there was a great, gnawing hunger of the spirit. This feeling of emptiness eventually drove me to the
point of despair. At last, one night I felt so drained that I
tried to gas myself. I was full of remorse for the things I
had left undone, especially in relation to my mother. I
felt I had been left totally bereft by her death.

As I lay there with my head in the gas oven, the Lord
spoke clearly to me: 'Martin, I have not taken you out of
one gutter to put you into another'. I got up quickly,
turned off the gas and opened all the windows. It

seemed that something similar was happening within me. I was opening windows and doors that had been bolted and barred for so long against fresh air and light. I got down on my knees and cried and prayed for a long time. I just asked the Lord to take complete charge of my life, to do with me whatever He wished to do.

Shortly after that, I went along to a special Mass for healing in Glenmaroon Convent. What a liberating, transforming experience that was for me. During the Lord's prayer, the people on either side of me took my hands. The tears just streamed down my face. I felt I was being washed clean inside and out. As the beautiful chorus of tongue-singing welled up around me, I thanked the Lord for all the people there.

I thought the following Wednesday would never come. Indeed, after every prayer meeting it was the same. I could not get enough of the prayerful atmosphere, the fellowship, the love and support and the sharing of gifts and griefs. I've not missed the weekly prayer meeting since – in nearly five years. For me, much of the healing came about through forgiving and coming to understand that the people – especially the priests and nuns whom I felt had wronged and humiliated me – were victims of their past just as much as I was. I met some wonderful priests and nuns at the prayer meetings and at the healing Masses. They ministered lovingly to me in my hunger for the food of the gospel. They taught me about the Baptism in the Spirit and they prayed with me for the release of the Holy Spirit. My life has not been the same since.

God has blessed me in so many ways, materially and spiritually. I now run two garages in Dublin. I have been involved in doing a lot of retreat work in schools, and hope to form a School's Retreat Team. I lead the Glenmaroon Youth Prayer Meeting, which meets in Chapelizod every Tuesday night. God has put into me a deep love of prayer and of the Scriptures. I remember once, after a meeting, sitting up till four one morning with a friend, talking about the gospel and the mercy and love of Jesus. When I got home, I had a wonderful experience. I was making a sandwich when all at once I had a vivid sense of the presence of Jesus there in the kitchen. 'Lord,' I cried, 'it is true what Mary said. You are not in the tomb. You have truly risen!' I just knew in that wonderful moment that the Lord had answered every prayer I had ever made in my lifetime. All that, in spite of my sinfulness, my infidelity and even the times that I blasphemed against Him. He had been watching the way my life had been going downhill. He was there in those times of loneliness and dejection since my childhood. He had indeed gone before me to prepare a place for me.

Now I can look forward eagerly to the New Jerusalem of the Book of Revelation. I used to have an inordinate fear of death. Now I eagerly look forward to the promise of the Lord that when He calls me there will be no more sadness, no more mourning and every tear will be wiped away. On that day 'every knee shall bow and every tongue confess that Jesus Christ is Lord'.

Lord Jesus, I thank You and praise Your holy name. I thank You for the gift of life. I thank You for the gift of sobriety, for the gift of freedom. I praise and bless Your name. Amen.

17

GOD WAS UP TO SOMETHING

SR. BRIGID DUNNE

Sr. Brigid leads a House of Prayer in Cork and co-ordinates various interdenominational activities in Cork. She serves on the National Service Committee for Catholic Charismatic Renewal.

I was born in England into a Roman Catholic family, a family that was truly committed and active in church affairs. Looking back, I can see that God was very real to all my family and I was given a good grounding in the things of the Lord. I was seven years old when my mother died and it was my father's sister who reared me and my two younger sisters. We could have had a disturbed childhood, for things were very hard in those post-war days, but we realise, my sisters and I, that there was so much love in this extended family – Uncle and Granny were there too – that it saw us through many difficulties and troubles. Prayer was always an important part of our daily lives and I never remember grumbling about going to church, as so many children do! It was fun to sing in the choir. My father was choirmaster and I came to love Gregorian chant in particular, a love that is with me still.

I grew up with strong Christian values and at eighteen I left home to start my training as a religious sister. I was very young when I first heard the call to become a nun and I never really deflected from my purpose. I had always felt that the Lord wanted me to give my life to

Him in this way, serving Him in my brothers and sisters in the Church. I went to France for three years for my novitiate training as a La Retraite sister. They were tough years, but very happy ones. I came to know the Lord in a deeper way and was prepared for service in whatever way He would lead.

In 1960 I made my vows and returned to England, to Weston-Super-Mare, where I was asked to look after the catering for the school. After a year I was sent to Salisbury, again to do the catering for the school and, of course, the community. Those were the years before and after the Second Vatican Council – things were changing in the Catholic Church and religious life, too, was changing quite rapidly. They were challenging and sometimes very difficult times. I was no longer quite sure where life was going, but I still was determined to continue to follow the Lord, wherever He might lead.

During this time I returned to France and prepared to make my final commitment in La Retraite. This I did in 1966 and returned to Salisbury to continue my work there. These were times of growing openness among ourselves and between the different Churches. I was aware that God was 'up to something'. Something more was on offer, something more was to be discovered.

Then I was posted to Birmingham in 1970, to a retreat house, where I had the job of bursar. One day someone I had met only once before invited me to come to a prayer meeting. I remember this as an extraordinary moment – suddenly I recognised that this was 'it', though I had yet to discover what 'it' really was! I had heard a call from the Lord. Somehow I knew that this was what I had been seeking, without even knowing it. Somehow time stood still and when it started again things were never to be quite the same ever again.

I went along to the prayer meeting and found a group of about a dozen people, Catholics and Protestants, who prayed together spontaneously and praised the Lord and listened to His Word. I felt at home. I was at ease. I recog-

nised I had come to the beginning of a new journey. I
was happy to start out on it, not really realising where it
might lead me, but knowing that God was in it and calling me to follow Him in a newer, deeper way. I got
involved in what was happening and I have stayed
involved ever since, in what came to be known as
Charismatic Renewal.

After a couple of years in Renewal I found I had to
make choices about continuing to serve the prayer
groups or to take another road, making attendance at
prayer meetings difficult. In 1972 I had been transferred
to London and had continued my involvement with the
prayer groups, and especially with the monthly Days of
Renewal. But where was the Lord leading me?

I went away with some of the group for a weekend. I
had been suffering from recurring back pain from disc
lesions, the result of a fall in my teens, and eventually the
pain had become constant and unremitting. The group
prayed with me and the pain vanished. I remember my
first reaction was to exclaim: 'I can feel my toes!' And
then I burst into song in tongues! How could I leave a
group where the Lord was so obviously working? I felt
He was showing me the way ahead – commitment to His
work through the Spirit in Renewal. But it was not to be
with the group in London, for soon after this, in 1973, I
was sent to Ireland.

I took up my duties in La Retraite in Cork, once more
looking after the catering and accounts. Within six days
of arriving I had found a prayer meeting and I got
involved very quickly in all that was going on. Those
were early days in Renewal and we had so much to
learn. One of the charisms of La Retraite sisters is to help
people to pray. But I also found that my brothers and sisters in the groups were helping me to grow more and
more in my friendship with the Lord. And in those early
days we often gathered across the denominational
divides and found we had much to share and learn from
each other and I found, too, that when we did reach out

to each other across the seeming divides, the Lord blessed us more powerfully. I remember with joy how the Lord healed me, a Catholic, of an ear complaint, when prayed over by a Presbyterian minister at a healing service in a Methodist church. I would need to write a book to chronicle all the deeds of the Lord in my life since then! Perhaps one day I will!

The numbers coming to meetings continued to grow and the number of groups increased too. There were so many people needing help. As a Church we had prayed for a fresh outpouring of the Spirit, a New Pentecost – and we had got it! And now we had to find ways of helping each other to grow in this life in the Spirit.

I found that more and more people were coming to talk to me, asking me to pray with them for healing, guidance, strength, growth in their prayer life. It was difficult sometimes to get my work done, feeding the students in the hostel, doing the accounts. Once more there were choices to be made. Where was the Lord leading this time? Others, too, were seeing needs and trying to find ways of meeting them. We thought that perhaps a place might be set up where people could come to find and give all sorts of help.

Then I was asked by my superiors to take time out for further study and I went to England for a while for this, returning to Cork in 1980. It was that year that some of us set up a Prayer Centre. We were offered the use of a hall in the old Presbyterian church in the city centre and La Retraite freed me from most other duties so that I could give time to working there. From the start, the venture was an interdenominational one and we worked and prayed together, helping each other and whoever came seeking help, or prayer, or growth in the Spirit. We stayed there nine years and I can say that during that time I grew in my friendship with the Lord more and more. I also grew in my relationships with other people, as our fellowship in the Lord deepened and became ever more real. There were difficult times as well, for we are human beings and we don't always get things right. We had to learn tolerance and forgiveness and understanding, seeking ways to sort out our differences and repenting of the ways in which we hurt each other. The painful times can be sources of growth, too.

During this time I grew very fond of the minister of the church and his wife, the Rev Eric and Mrs Roz May. They have since gone home to the Lord, but they had become a very important part of the fabric of my life and I thank God for them, for their generosity and openness, their kindness and their deep sense of prayer. The constant support I felt from them was very real and they have truly been a blessing in my life.

Then, for various reasons, we had to find other premises and in 1990 reopened the Prayer Centre in North Main Street where I am still serving the Lord and my brothers and sisters. One of the ways in which I see the Lord at work is through the Life in the Spirit seminars. I have been giving these seminars for many years now, several times each year. It is a privilege to see the growth in the things of the Lord in so many people, as their faith is deepened, as they find the Bible come alive for them, as they recommit their lives to Jesus and resolve to live according to his way.

Life as a Catholic has changed a lot and life as a religious has changed even more over these years, and I know that in the years to come this pattern of change is certainly going to continue. Yet, through it all, the constant presence of the Lord has been my joy and mainstay. God is still 'up to something' and He still calls us to reach out to Him and to each other. I intend doing just that until He calls me home!

18

THE NIGHT MY SON DIED
GEORGE MCAULIFFE

*Married to Sheila, George McAuliffe, from Co. Kerry is
a 58-year-old maths teacher and Deputy Head of school.
Six children: Muireann (working in the Financial Services
Centre in Dublin), Emir (a social worker in Tralee),
Joe (a doctor in Cork), Deirdre (a microbiologist, studying in
University College Dublin), Aoife and John (both students).*

As I look back on my life, moments of significance stand
out. For the most part, the implications of these moments
were not immediately apparent. One occurred on March
20th, 1973. I came in from teaching at school to find my
little son David very sick and complaining of a pain in
his back. I somehow knew, almost immediately, that my
walk on earth would never be the same again; it was
make-or-break time. With a heavy, dark foreboding, I
sensed something major was around the corner. My wife
Sheila and I turned that corner within a few days, when
we were told that a cancerous growth had caused
David's kidney to collapse, and his life would be short.
The pain was as if knives were being twisted within us
as we watched 'our little man' deteriorate, till finally his
sufferings came to an end on November 14th, 1973.

In the months of his sickness, strange and unexpected
things began to happen to me. It is important to state
now that, as I lived through those days, the suggestion
that I might one day be sharing or, wonder of wonders,
even writing about them, would have been dismissed by
me as absurd. It also needs to be said that the tragedy in

our lives would not warrant a footnote in the book of pain in this land of ours. My story is not about a great tragedy, but about a great transition from a place of meaninglessness and alienation to one of purpose, peace, joy and belonging. One of these strange experiences that puzzled me took place during the summer of 1973. As I walked the streets of Cork, pondering over the events that had invaded our lives, it was as if a voice from above said to me 'The North of Ireland will know about this'. Those words like a star, occasionally visible mostly invisible, have remained with me ever since. But in 1973 the North, for me, was a faraway land, occupied by an enemy people who were thwarting our rightful entitlement to a 'thirty-two-county' Republic.

From childhood, the two great causes that I had pledged myself to were Catholicism and Republicanism – understandably so, since I had been born into a home where my mother faithfully practised Catholicism and my father, as an original IRA man, who fought the British before independence, had been excommunicated in the service of Republicanism. 'Isms' ruled my life. From a very young age, I craved for an understanding of the purpose of life, and in particular *my* life. However, in the climate of my youth there was no understanding for me. I accepted simplistically that Catholicism was necessary to make provision for the next life, and Republicanism was the only political road that promised glory in this life. The fact that to accept one I had to assent to 'mysteries' and to serve the other I might have to kill or be killed, only added to my confusion. I didn't know who I was, where I came from, what I was doing on earth, or where I was going. I just had to disregard these questions, in the belief that there were no satisfactory answers.

During the mid 1950s I associated with militant groupings and openly canvassed for Sinn Fein, in opposition to the wishes of my father, who was then an ardent supporter of Fianna Fail. My most notable success in the political arena was to convince my mother and aunt to vote as I wanted, a fact they had to conceal from my father and uncle for the rest of their lives. But the 'campaign' died and, in the late 1950s, I found myself in a seminary for the training of priests, offering myself to serve Catholicism in darkest Africa. During those years I made many good friends and had no difficulty with my studies. But I still had no inner peace or certainty about anything, and I left that seminary, with 'the movement of my thought not arrested', the door to glory on the political front closed, and facing an absurd life.

I went back to university, and to drink, with all its related excesses. I qualified as a teacher, got a job in Milltown, Co. Kerry, and met a beautiful girl, Sheila, whom I wisely pursued and courted till she agreed to marry me. By 1973 we had two children, Muireann and David. Life was still a long absurd road ahead, at the end of which lay an even more absurd phenomenon called death. I had a crippling dread of death, produced by my awareness of how far short I fell in every way of the standards the Church said were necessary for salvation. But in 1973 the death I was now awaiting was not my own, but that of my much loved and loving son, David.

It became obvious very soon that the planet earth didn't even pretend to claim that it could help us when we were first told about his cancer. The only one I had heard of who had made claims to be able to help in all circumstances was the one called Jesus Christ, though, for myself, I had no experience of such help. To me, He was a dead hero who lived 2,000 years ago, but was, unfortunately, somehow still somewhere in the vicinity putting together a dreaded judgment on my life.

Cornered by circumstances, driven by love for my little boy, I turned to the God of the Christians in a serious, determined way. Within a few weeks, an extraordinary peace, like liquid love, fell into my life, a 'peace the world doesn't understand'. With that peace came joy and excitement and a realisation that for the first time in

my life I was communicating with God as a living, loving person. This Jesus was alive. I was finally making
contact with reality. As I held David while his breathing
ceased at 8.49 p.m. on the night of November 14th,
everything in me cried out to keep him in my arms. But
deep down I knew that through this deep pain I was
looking at a beginning rather than an end. Deeper than
that grief was this joy and peace that even death could
not dispel. The fact that this Jesus was alive dominated
my horizon completely. Death lost its power to terrorise
me. My life did have a purpose. Peace and joy filled my
heart. There was, after all, in spite of, and maybe even
because of, the great pain, an exciting future for David
on the other side of death, and for myself and Sheila on
this side.

In that future which we embraced lay many wonderful revelations from Scripture that Christ, His work on
earth complete, our great High Priest, is sending once
again His Holy Spirit, in the words of John XXIII, 'as in a
new Pentecost'. That future was to hold a deep peace
and joy in the midst of many difficulties and dark days.
That future held the fulfilment of that 'word' I heard in
1973: 'The North of Ireland will know about this'. In
these intervening years, through developments totally
unconnected with any efforts or strivings on my part, I
have been privileged to witness to the good news of salvation through Jesus Christ throughout the entire North,
from Mountain Lodge to Long Kesh, from Castlederg to
Belfast. As a teacher of mathematics, with a mind that
craves and needs certainty and with an almost sacred
obligation not to link David's death with any question-
able claims, I can, and do, with a clear conscience, bold-
ly say that something new is happening. A living God is
reaching out to all, to bless and to save.

On Good Friday 1974, at a meeting of about eighty
people, I had an extraordinary experience. At the start of
the service, after the crowd had just taken their seats, the
awesomeness and wonder of what Jesus had achieved

on my behalf on that first Good Friday hit me with such force and clarity that I stood to my feet and declared aloud, again and again, to everyone: 'I'm saved! I'm saved!' It seemed appropriate to stand. Those two words 'I'm saved!' reflected the revelation I was at that point receiving. I had never heard of this phenomenon, and the term 'saved', which I later heard in the North of Ireland, was up to that moment totally foreign to me. I think of it as if, on that day, I tied one end of a piece of elastic to Calvary and I hold the other end fixed in my heart. Wherever I go or whatever I say, I am drawn back to the glorious victory of that first Good Friday.

Later that year, I read from time to time in the papers about this strange phenomenon of speaking in tongues. I had read of this in the Bible and had studied it as a piece of ancient church history. Now the possibility that I, in the twentieth century, could have this experience of the early Christians excited my interest greatly, and I longed for more of this 'power from above'. I had decided not to set limits to the 'invasion' of God and His truth into my life, now that the old 'reliables' and old 'certainties' had given way to new and exciting challenges and a dynamic relationship with Jesus Christ.

At a meeting in Dublin, with many around me praying and praising the Lord in unfamiliar words, I raised my hands up and said something like 'Here goes, Lord, tongues or bust'. At that instant I felt a great release of power and peace and out of my mouth came this torrent of new words that I had never learned. The 'great brain' that I had imagined was the only instrument with which to understand spiritual truth was, in a way, being bypassed in a new and different way of knowing my Heavenly Father, and I was speaking in a very special way with Him. However, I was sensible enough to know that man's capacity for self-delusion is great. I had studied psychology at university and knew there was a need to test everything. The yardsticks I used were the Bible and the judgement of wise people. Having tested everything thus, the only conclusion I could arrive at was that, contrary to the testimony and wish of the world, Jesus Christ was in fact pouring out His Spirit again as in the days of the early Church, and I, totally undeservedly, was a beneficiary of such an outpouring. I was living a new kind of life. I had a new awareness and understanding. I was under new management. I was 'born again'.

This is but a very inadequate account of my story, but I pray that the living Father might use it in some little way. I will have failed if I have communicated any other message than that Jesus Christ is alive, that He is Lord, to the glory of God the Father.

19

DIVINE APPOINTMENTS
REV RONNIE MITCHEL

*Rev Ronnie Mitchel was born in Belfast and was a civil
servant before entering the Montfort Missionary Society.
He was ordained a Catholic priest in 1973. He is currently
based at Montfort House, Monaghan, Ireland and has a
retreat-giving ministry. He has worked in England and
Scotland and was novice master for his Society
for seven years. His first book on the theme of
'The Church In the Power of the Spirit' is expected
to be published early in 1998.*

Have you noticed how God sends people into your life to
bless you? I have found this truth in a number of 'divine
appointments' with Protestant brothers and sisters. I
have been drawn deeper into the Lord's saving love
through such relationships. Here I witness to the value of
such encounters for my own Christian life and ministry.

Early times . . .
It really started with a 'God-incidence'. I met Catholic
Bishop Joseph McKinney from the United States. It was
an autumn day in 1974. The venue was the busy
Heathrow Airport, London. Seeing I was in priestly garb,
he approached and struck up a conversation.

The Bishop was travelling to speak at a conference in
the RDS Hall, Dublin. I was on my way to take up a
pastoral appointment in Montfort House, Monaghan. He
mentioned Larry, whom I knew from Belfast Legion of

Mary days. When I arrived in Belfast, I contacted Larry and we set off for the conference the following weekend.

On the Sunday morning, a Church of Ireland minister, Rev Cecil Kerr, taught about and prayed for the baptism of the Holy Spirit. This is the grace of being able to witness more powerfully to the presence of Jesus in one's life. I had never heard of it. I could accept it with my head but I needed an experience of it to believe.

The experience came in triplicate: wind, water and fire! It happened at the Catholic Mass in the chapel at Belfield Campus, that never-to-be-forgotten Sunday afternoon. O Happy Day!

The same Bishop McKinney, after Holy Communion, spoke of Thomas touching the wounds of Christ (John 20:27). I saw myself in that scene, with the Precious Blood upon my hands too. I then felt a shiver go down my spine, as if I was wonderfully cleansed inside and a fire enkindled within me. I experienced the force of Cardinal Newman's argument, that we come to a living faith in Jesus more through imagination and grace than through concept and reason.

The effect of this experience on my own life, ministry and relationships was to become truly transforming. All my baptismal, confirmation and ordination graces suddenly surfaced. I discovered that ministry was letting God work through me. It is a privilege, a joy to be Catholic and a priest.

It is significant also to honour St Louis Marie de Montfort, the seventeenth-century founder of our Missionary Congregation. I now see clearly how his spirituality and means of total consecration to Christ is part of God's plan for the salvation of the human race.

One of the consequences of this deepened awareness of 'The Power of Pentecost' in my life was a great openness to Protestants who professed Jesus as Lord and sought fellowship in the Spirit. In these 'divine appointments', adherence to a particular Christian tradition was not an obstacle. This led me to focus on what we agreed on, rather than what kept us apart. There was a glorious unity in diversity.

I realised that I had held a lot of mistaken notions about Protestants. My upbringing on the Falls Road in Belfast had kept me apart from them. I remember during my time in the Northern Ireland Civil Service, how I was once 'told off' for sharing faith with 'our separated brethren'. My theological education had only enabled me to meet them occasionally, and then at an academic level.

And so it continued

At that 1974 Dublin Conference I met Mark Nolan – now a Benedictine priest in Bec Abbey, France. I had known Mark for years, as his family had lived beside us. He had been attending meetings led by an Englishman called Keith Gerner at Hollywood, which is just outside Belfast. Keith welcomed Catholics, and I went with Mark. Here I found the Scriptures opened in a way I had never before experienced.

Here at Keith's we met other Pentecostal preachers who had such obvious love for the Lord. There was Sandy Thompson, an Irish evangelist who had lived in Jerusalem and had a word of knowledge ministry. Then there was Bill Turner, from Staffordshire, England, with a prophetic and vision ministry. Nor could I ever forget American Michael McKerricher, with a dynamic preaching ministry. I thought such gifts had died out with the early Church. How wrong I was! These men could speak (without notes) for an hour, and no one was bored.

There was good teaching at further National Conferences in Dublin with Anglicans, Fr. Michael Harper from England and Archbishop Bill Burnett of Cape Town, South Africa. At Belfast gatherings, I was blessed by listening to the ministry of the Word from David McKee, Terry Fullam and David Matthews, each of whom spoke from their own tradition.

Though years have passed, I still remember vividly

the Christ-centred message of the Rev David Watson, an
Anglican priest, in St Anne's Cathedral, Belfast. I went
home convicted. What preaching! What power! There
was such a clear exposition of God's Word, demanding
decision. How we need such ministry in our Churches
today! It can be so easy to preach an outward form of
religion and yet neglect its inner power.

I attended the International Fountain Trust Conferences in London, where I heard Tom Smail, Colin Urquhart
and Don Double. I even heard Dr Paul Yonggi Cho at the
Assemblies of God Conference in Minehead, England.

I was later to become associated with Paul Kyle and
the Community of Christ the King (which was mostly
Protestant). We held summer camps in Ballycastle and
Donegal. Through these I came to understand more
clearly evangelical values, especially fellowship. From
Paul, also, I grasped the power of singing and music to
touch our deepest emotions in worship.

I regularly meet at different venues with other
Christians for fellowship, teaching, sharing and reconciliation. The focus is on what God is doing and wants to
do in healing the sectarian wounds of division in our
land. Here I find my Catholic identity acknowledged
and honoured. I would also add that it is the Protestants,
who have been touched by this spiritual renewal, who
are life-giving to me.

Perhaps ironically, the exposure to such devoted
Protestant Christians has opened up to me more the 'hidden' treasures of my own Catholic faith, especially the
sacraments and the role of institutional authority.
Incidentally, I can see the saints now as those who powerfully used their 'spiritual gifts' .

And what lies ahead . . .
How could such 'divine appointments' bless you and me
for the future? I see undeveloped potential in the following areas.

1. Relationships

I have discovered, through meeting and praying with other Christians, a greater sense of what it means to be a member of the Body of Christ. The word 'fellowship' is now a reality. Ministry is now a service. It is allowing the Holy Spirit to draw us together in faith, hope and love. It is acknowledging the truth that only a person with a loving heart can create community. It is believing Pope John XXIII's prayer for a 'New Pentecost'.

How then are we to build up the Body of Christ in its local setting? Be more responsible, be more committed, use the spiritual gifts, grow in prayer and knowledge of the Word of God, enjoy life-giving worship, be interdependent, reach out more to others, be forgiving.

2. The Church

The spiritual and the institutional sides of the Church need one another. The lack of balance and harmony here has profoundly weakened the Church's life and mission.

Without the Spirit, the Church risks becoming a corpse. Without authority, the Church is like a river without banks. Catholics and Protestants can learn from each other.

Leadership at all levels is a charism for service operating under the anointing of the Holy Spirit, and in love (1 Cor 12:31).

3. Ministry

New ministries, such as praying spontaneously with others for personal or community needs, can be fostered. New life and importance has to be breathed into the old ministries e.g. preaching. Training for evangelisation is a priority. We need those who will 'model' for us new forms of ministry and community. As I think of those who have most influenced me, I often wonder whose 'mantles' I am wearing! We are in exciting times.

4. Divine providence

This is a favourite theme of Montfort. This sense of God's

provision for every need was wonderfully heightened for me when Mark Nolan and I visited for a week the Protestant Sisterhood of Mary in Darmstadt, Germany. There we saw at first hand how God's Fatherly love provided spiritual and material miracles for this infant community which, being born out of the throes of World War II, undertook a ministry of reconcilation in a deep spirit of repentance.

This experience was to powerfully shape my own spiritual vision for reconciliation in Ireland. The Christian Renewal Centre in Rostrevor, Co. Down has caught this vision in a very special way and there Protestants and Catholics pray and work together for the healing of this land.

5. The transforming power of praise and worship
At a conference in Belfast in the mid-seventies I learnt one of the controlling lessons of my life. It was a public prophetic word from a Protestant girl, Hazel McEvoy: 'Praise is both the work and the weapon.' I found many spiritual victories flowed, many 'strongholds' were uprooted out of this tremendous word. Praise gives worship its dynamic quality to change our lives and bless others.

6. Outreach
My theology became permeated and set on fire by the Holy Spirit. In these 'divine encounters' I could experience a hunger for the Lord and an outreach for prodigals that enkindled my own missionary spirit. The Church lives to witness powerfully to the moving events of Christ's life, death and resurrection in a world that is hungry for the inner freedom of the human spirit.

'So if the Son makes you free, you will be free indeed' (John 8:36).

20

SAY YOU HATE JESUS OR I'LL KILL YOU

PADDY MONAGHAN

Paddy is a Catholic lay missionary and business consultant, from Dun Laoghaire. He is involved in promoting renewal in the Catholic Church, in fostering reconciliation among Christians and in building Jewish/Christian relationships.

Should I die before the Lord returns, I would like the inscription on my tombstone to read, 'He was a friend of God'. One of the names by which God has revealed himself, is Jehovah Rophe (which means God Our Shepherd or God Our Friend).

I am forty-six years old and live near Dun Laoghaire. I am married to Anne and have four lovely children – Ruth Anne, John, David and Andrew. I work part of my week as a financial consultant in my own small business and the rest of the week as an Evangelical Catholic lay missionary and reconciliation co-ordinator. As an Evangelical Catholic I am concerned to see a Christ-centred, biblically-based renewal in the Catholic Church, foster reconciliation among Christians and build up Jewish–Christian relationships.

I grew up in the lovely town of Kells, Co. Meath, made famous by the priceless Book of Kells, the book of the Four Gospels illustrated by Columba's monks and now one of our national treasures. Prayer was an integral part of our home life – family prayers were regarded as an important duty. One of my playmates was from a Church of Ireland family, and I often wondered why he went to a different school. At that stage of my life I thought there were three different types of people in the world – men, women and priests.

I was inordinately shy. I had buck teeth, and paid the price for it through endless teasing from my peers. Again and again, the pitiless song 'All he wants for Christmas is his two front teeth' echoed in my ears. In secondary school, anything that drew attention to me, such as coming top of the class in a test, caused me extreme embarrassment. I remember pinching myself when someone told a joke, to stop myself from laughing, in case I attracted attention. My self-consciousness was a blight on my life.

At eighteen years of age, a shy, introverted country boy, I went, in great trepidation, to University College, Dublin to do a commerce degree. I joined a Catholic lay organisation called the Legion of Mary, whose members engaged in various forms of charitable work. My weekly task was to visit mentally handicapped people in St Vincent's, on the Navan Road in Dublin, which I found very enjoyable and rewarding.

I lived for three years in a bed-sit in Santry in north Dublin. For the first year I was very insecure as a person, while defensively putting on an outward show of being an extrovert. I felt that I had no one to really talk to and share how stupid and inadequate I felt at times. I can remember having a sheet of paper stuck up on the wall in my bed-sit with three words written on it that summarised what I felt to be most lacking in my life: Security, Trust, Confidence. I did not have any inner security, didn't trust people and had little or no confidence in myself.

This all changed when, in the course of my work with the mentally handicapped, I met a fellow student called Ann and we fell in love. I suddenly had a friend – someone with whom I could share anything, especially situations which left me feeling embarrassed and silly. I developed real security, started to trust people and grew in confidence in myself. Only later did we both come to know Jesus as our Lord and Saviour – the source of love. This was in February 1973.

For the previous year, a group of us in UCD had been meeting together to study the Scriptures, but I didn't feel it was really making any major impact on my life. Then, in December 1972, I attended a Liberation Theology Workshop in York University, along with fifteen or twenty students from UCD. In the course of our time there, we found ourselves invited to a 'charismatic' prayer meeting. This was my first encounter with people praying spontaneously in public. I was deeply touched.

We came back to UCD and decided to start a charismatic prayer group. I found it tough going at first, but I persisted in going to six or seven prayer meetings. Then, towards the end of February 1973, it happened! I found the Lord for myself. I was born again by the Spirit of God and simultaneously baptised in His Holy Spirit. It was as if all along I had been in a dark room, and suddenly the light was switched on! I remember waking up in my bed-sit in Rathmines and knowing something had changed. I picked up the Bible and the words just seemed to jump out at me. It was no longer just the inspired, authoritative Word of God, it was now His love letter to me. I could hardly leave it down. I was just so overwhelmed with the consciousness of God's love for me personally.

I remember cycling into university that morning, singing the praises of God. I met a university porter on the way in and he said to me, 'Good morning Paddy, you look so happy you must be in love!' I said, 'Yes!' I didn't tell him that the love that filled me was not for a girl but for the Lord. I had given my whole life to Jesus to take and use in any way He wanted.

Some time later, my commitment to Christ was

violently put to the test. I had moved to share a house with three other students, who were also Evangelical Catholics. On the request of a priest friend we were giving temporary accommodation to a young man who had just been released from Mountjoy Jail. Since my room was the largest, I was voted the privilege of sharing it with him. After about three months, I came home one day to find him in a drunken state, manifesting what I later realised was demonic behaviour and terrorising the others.

With my Bible in one hand, I confronted him. He snatched the Bible from me and tore it in two. Then, with superhuman strength, he pinned me to the wall, pulled out a knife, pressed it against my throat and shouted 'Say you hate Jesus, or I'll kill you right now!' I was terrified. I knew he had been imprisoned for causing grievous bodily harm and that he fully intended to carry out his threat. Unaccountably, there suddenly flashed before my eyes a headline in the following morning's *Irish Times*: 'Charismatic Murdered in Mount Merrion!' Yet somehow, by the grace of God, through gritted teeth, I said, 'I love Jesus!' He went to kill me, but suddenly seemed to freeze, and the knife dropped from his hand. Immediately he fell to the floor, weeping because he had turned on a friend, and he had to be restrained from using the knife on himself. He later told me that he had taken part in a satanic ritual that day and was under the influence of the devil. He had wanted to kill me, but when I declared my love for Jesus he said that some powerful force caught hold of his wrist and he was powerless to drive the knife home. I believe that was a divine intervention. Recalling David Wilkerson's *The Cross and the Switchblade*, I pointed out to my friend that he had just had a demonstration of the fact that the cross of Jesus was more powerful than the switchblade. Since that time I have feared nothing. I know that my Redeemer lives, and that whatever seeks to come against me must pass Him first.

One of the first things I prayed about after being brought to this personal knowledge of Jesus was whether I should become a Catholic priest. That was the only way I knew in which a full commitment to Jesus could find expression within the Catholic tradition. I prayed and sought the Lord for two full weeks on this and God answered me very clearly. I began to notice that as the Catholic chaplains, who were my good friends, met with some of the many students on the periphery of church life, the students tended not to relate honestly to them, but rather put up a front. The clerical collar seemed to pose a major barrier to real communication. I felt the Lord telling me that this was not His way for me.

I had received a first-class honours degree in Commerce and was now in the middle of a Master's degree in Business Studies, specialising in finance. As I asked the Lord for guidance, I had a strong conviction that my 'mission field' was to be in Ireland. I came to realise that my discipleship training programme for this mission field would lie in finishing my Master's degree and going into the business world. When this became clear I received the peace of the Lord to complete the course, and was duly awarded the degree. I then worked in a Merchant Bank in Dublin – the National Irish Investment Bank – for five years and then in the Industrial Development Authority for a further two years. During this time I got married to a lovely Christian woman that God brought into my life, also called Anne, which means 'grace'. God had surely shown his grace to me.

One of the significant things that profoundly affected my life, one year after my conversion, was attending a conference in Limerick of Evangelical Catholics and Evangelical Protestants from the North and South of Ireland, sponsored by the Full Gospel Businessmen's Fellowship. During the worship time, Sister Alphonsus, an Evangelical Catholic nun from Portadown, shared a prophetic picture, which portrays, I believe, God's plan

and purpose for Ireland. In this picture she saw a map of
Ireland. Logs were brought from the North down to the
centre, and oil from the South was poured on them. Fire
came down from the clouds and set the whole pile
ablaze. The fire then swept the length and breadth of
Ireland, until the whole land was aflame. It then covered
England, Scotland and Wales and Continental Europe.

She paused for a moment and then shared the inter-
pretation that God had given her. The logs, she said, represented the Evangelical Protestants, who were steeped
in the Word of God from knee high, but who, without
the baptism of the Holy Spirit, could become hard and
legalistic. The oil, she said, represented the born again,
baptised in the Holy Spirit Roman Catholics, now full of
a zealousness for God, but lacking a foundation in the
Word of God. As God would bring the two together, so
Holy Spirit revival would sweep Ireland and Ireland
would again become a light to the nations. This profoundly impacted me and I said to the Lord, 'I don't
want to be involved in something that's "oil" only and I
don't want to be involved in something that's "logs"
only, but would you use me to bring the logs and the oil
together?' And God has taken me at my word.

Over these last twenty-four years, I have been
involved in bringing the logs and oil together in Ireland.
I believe this is God's vision for Ireland. It was one of the
basic incentives that led me, with others, to set up the
'Evangelical Catholic Initiative' (ECI). ECI is comprised
of Catholic Christians who are evangelical by conviction
(i.e. who have accepted the evangel – the good news of
salvation through Jesus Christ – and who seek to live
under his Lordship in accordance with the teachings of
Scripture). We seek to promote the Kingdom of God
through working, under the guidance and empowering
of the Holy ,for a Christ-centred, biblically-based renewal in the Roman Catholic Church. We also seek to foster
reconciliation among Christians and to build up relationships between Christians and Jews. We see   recon-

ciliation between the Christian Churches and renewal within the Christian Churches as being two sides of the same coin. I believe with all my heart that it's only as born again Christians find one another, the logs finding the oil, across the denominational divide, across barriers, not just of doctrine, but of history, language, culture and politics, that Holy Spirit revival will again sweep Ireland. As 2 Chronicles 7:14 says, 'If my people, who are called by my name, will humble themselves and pray and seek my face and turn from their wicked ways, then I will hear from heaven, forgive their sin and heal their land.'

I have been very much involved in reconciliation in Northern Ireland over the years. I regularly pray for the Lord's protection on the RUC and have attended a number of RUC funerals over the years. Two incidents among many stand out. When three RUC constables were blown up just outside Newry, I brought flowers to the RUC Station in Newry on behalf of Catholic Christians in Dublin – they were deeply moved by this gesture. Another time when the IRA attacked an RUC station in another border town, a colleague and myself arrived at the station with flowers and asked to speak to the RUC officer in charge. He came and met us and was so deeply moved that he started to cry. He then confided in us that he was a Catholic and he had to go to a different Catholic church each week to participate in the Eucharist, to avoid the danger of being ambushed. My heart went out to him and we prayed with him for the Lord's protection on him. In June 1997 I attended the funerals of two Community RUC men, cruelly assassinated in Lurgan, Co. Armagh. Both men were committed Christians and their families appreciated my attendance. May God grant that they are the last RUC officers to be murdered by the IRA.

I have seen, again and again, how bridges can be built, even in such a deeply divided community, through the sharing of one's testimony. For many months, a group of Loyalists had picketed the weekly evening Mass at Harryville, a suburb of Ballymena, Co. Antrim. In January 1997 Mr Robert Saulters, the Grand Master of the Orange Order, and eleven senior officials of the Order came to stand with the Catholic community at Harryville in condemnation of the picketing. It was probably a new experience for him to be called a Lundy and a traitor by some of the Loyalist picketers. I had the privilege, along with a colleague, of welcoming him to Harryville. I then asked him if he was a born again Christian – he was surprised at such a question coming from a Catholic. He said that at sixteen years of age he had invited Jesus into his life. I then explained that I also was a born again Christian and shared my testimony with him. I then encouraged him, as Grand Master, to consider changing some aspects of the Orange Order that Catholics find offensive. This encounter with Mr Saulters led to a warm friendship. In June 1997 when a young Catholic man, Tom Hamill, was kicked to death by a group of Loyalists in Portadown, I attended his funeral. The night before, I talked to Mr Saulters and he asked me to convey his personal condolences to Mr Hamill's family and to the Catholic community in Portadown.

I have the privilege of serving on the Service Group of St Michael's Prayer and Bible Study in Dun Laoghaire. This meeting is interdenominational (logs and oil together!), and there is much blessing flowing from it. We have just completed our third Alpha Bible Study course, run jointly with the local Methodist church. We praise God that, as a result, some twenty people accepted Jesus as their Lord and Saviour. My hope and prayer is that, as the Word of God impacts the lives of more and more people, drawing them into a living relationship with Jesus Christ, we will see Ireland again becoming a land from which the gospel will go out powerfully to the nations.

21

HE TOUCHED ME

MARY O'ROURKE

*Mary teaches in Primary School and is a gifted
speaker at prayer and Bible study groups.*

I grew up in a large Catholic family, where prayer was
always an important part of family life. I went to a
Catholic school, and finally graduated from a Catholic
teacher training college. While my main teaching subject
was mathematics, I was also asked to teach religious
education. This was quite distressing for me, as I found
it very difficult to teach about God with any kind of conviction, because I was unsure of what I really believed
myself. When I discussed my dilemma with a priest, he
gave me some excellent advice, telling me not to pass on
my doubts to the young people entrusted to my charge.
I was not asked to teach my own ideas, but to confine
myself to teaching about a person, Jesus Christ.

My uncertainty at that time led me to ask many questions of others who demonstrated a strong faith. In my
quest for answers I read lots of books. Then my dad died
very suddenly. Though he had been ill for a long time,
we had not been expecting him to die. His death caught
me unprepared, and brought home to me how fragile life
was. I wondered where he had gone. I began to examine
my own life and assess my priorities. Then I read a little
book by Fr. John Powell, called *He Touched Me*, in which
he tells the story of his own life. He had worked as a
priest for a number of years before he realised that he did

not know the love of God in a personal way. In the book, he recounts the story of how God touched his life. I started to wonder if God could possibly touch my life also in that kind of personal way. It was a wonderful thought, but I did not have any real expectation that it could happen for me.

After teaching for seven years, I took a year out to study. During this time I met another teacher who was part of an interdenominational prayer group. We often talked about God. She kept inviting me along to the group, but I kept putting it off till 'next week', even though part of me wanted to go. I could see a peace and joy in my friend's life that was missing in mine. I knew, as she talked about Jesus in a personal way, that she really trusted God. Eventually, I decided to take the plunge and go with her.

A Presbyterian lady and a Catholic priest were in joint leadership of the group. During that first meeting, I felt uncomfortable with the emphasis on praise and extempore praying aloud. I was more accustomed to silent, contemplative prayer. I had never before witnessed the expression of the gifts of the Spirit, such as tongues and prophecy, as spoken of by Paul in his letters. It was all very strange to me, but there was no doubting the depth of genuine love coming from those people.

During the following week, various things that had been said at the meeting kept coming back to me, and I decided to go to another meeting. I had attended three meetings, listening to the joyful experiences of other people, when something wonderful happened in my own life. I suddenly awoke in the middle of the night, sensing that someone was calling my name, saying, 'Mary, Mary, I love you. You are precious to me.' I felt as if I was lying in a sea of love. I experienced the love of God touching my heart. He really touched me!

The next morning, I was so convinced of the reality of God's love that I wanted to stop everyone I met and tell them how much God loved them. Suddenly I saw everything in a different light. I felt His joy and new life within. I now knew with a strong heart-conviction that God really existed, that Jesus was really alive, that it was absolutely true that He had died for me. What measure of love! I couldn't stop talking about it, trying to bring home to people the immensity of God's love for them.

Shortly after this, I attended an interdenominational conference in Belfast on 'The Power of the Cross'. I was perplexed to see a group of Christians protesting outside the venue. They were unhappy with the idea of Protestants meeting together with Catholics to pray. They felt that this was displeasing to God. Inside the hall, my heart leapt as I heard the gospel proclaimed with great authority and power. I experienced the vibrant truth of those words from Hebrews 4: 'The word of God is living and active. Sharper than any double-edged sword . . . it judges the thoughts and attitudes of the heart.'

Afterwards, some people prayed with me and I had a fresh experience of God, of the release of the power and love of the Holy Spirit in my life. I wept with joy as I laid hold in a deeper way than ever of the fact that God did not condemn me but forgave me and accepted me. I understood as never before the 'power' of the cross. Jesus demolished the self-protective walls I had erected around my heart over the years. He poured his love and power in, so that I could let His love flow out to others. As God revealed His love and power to me, faith grew in my heart. For me, faith is a response to the revelation of God. He gave me a new desire to pray, to read His Word, to sing His praise and to follow Him. He gave fresh meaning to my life, gave me new purpose and changed my priorities.

One of the first words that came alive to me from the New Testament was in chapter 16 of John's Gospel: 'But when he, the Spirit of truth, comes, he will lead you into all truth.' I have come to experience this leading of the Holy Spirit many times since then. From the start, He planted an instinctive desire in my heart to be in close fellowship with other Christians, the kind of desire which must have motivated the early believers – as we see from the account of their lifestyle given in the second chapter of Acts. I joined a Catholic missionary grouping, involved in living and building Christian communities in school and parish settings in Canada. I spent two years there, before returning to Northern Ireland and becoming a member of an interdenominational community at the Christian Renewal Centre in Rostrevor. Here I shared in the life of the community for four years, as they prayed and worked for Church reconciliation and renewal.

I discovered that community living is never easy. It takes time to grow into a community, it demands patience and reliance upon God's grace. In community, I learned to listen, to forgive, to encourage, to share, to suffer with others, to love – in a word, to grow in Christ. I discovered wrong attitudes and prejudices in my own heart that I didn't realise were there. I had, for example, always had a problem with a certain flag-waving section of people in Northern Ireland who seemed to be forever shouting 'No Surrender!', no matter what was being proposed. Then the Lord showed me that I not infrequently had a 'No Surrender!' flag flying in my own heart, when I resisted doing something I knew He wanted me to do, or when I was so convinced of being right on certain issues that I refused to give space to the opinions of others. I had to start learning the secret of continually surrendering my will to His, in the knowledge that the vessel He fashions, He fills.

I know that God has a particular care for me as an individual, but His purpose for me is to be part of the Body of Christ, to live in close relationship with all others who believe in Him. Jesus Himself said that it is by the love we have for one another that others will know that we are His disciples. It therefore saddens me when some Christians express disappointment, when I share my journey in faith with them, at the fact that I have not left the Catholic Church. Some have even questioned whether I have really 'seen the light'. Yet God has put a love in my heart for the Catholic Church. I have experienced the sacraments of the Eucharist and Reconciliation as wonderful channels of healing. I do not feel threatened, but rather protected by the spiritual authority God has placed over me. I also love and respect other Christians who don't think like me. I deeply appreciate the friendships I have with many Protestant people, and the blessing they have been to me in my life.

So, by the grace of God, I continue to share the knowledge He has given me of Himself wherever He gives me opportunity. For me, there are often periods when such opportunities do not seem to arise, periods of apparent inactivity. But in these periods I am discovering something of what Mary must have experienced as she sat attentively at the feet of Jesus, while Martha was busy getting the meal ready. 'Mary has chosen what is better,' said Jesus. While often testing times, they are also precious times of invitation to enter into the experience of what was promised in Zephaniah 3:17: 'The Lord thy God in the midst of thee is mighty; he will save, he will rejoice over thee with joy; he will rest in his love, he will joy over thee with singing.' Through seasons of busyness and rest, of difficulty and contentment, He never fails to strengthen me in daily prayer to overcome failures and press on with living out the gospel in my relationships with family and friends and in my work situation. In every eventuality, He continues to demonstrate that His grace is sufficient for me.

22

A SCRIPTURE-CENTRED REVOLUTION

DAVID O'CONNOR

*David lectures in engineering in the University of Ulster
and is a leader in the Siloam Community
in North Belfast and active in building bridges
of hope across the community.*

I was brought up in a good Catholic family. I was raised by my father, but my grandmother, who had had thirteen children herself, also had a strong influence on my upbringing. It was a very loving home. God was very much part of the whole family's life and there was a strong consciousness of His reality. The fact that He was there for people in times of need was simply not questioned. We had the rosary every night, with plenty of 'trimmings'. I was always conscious of that little sneaky expectancy in the air that I would go on for the priesthood. It was that sort of traditional, pre-Vatican II Catholic home. I actually enjoyed going to the Friday and Sunday night devotions and confraternities.

I went to a boarding school and every day we had Mass in the early morning. I never found it a bother. That was during the sixties, the days of Vatican II, and I got it straight off the plate. My RE teacher was excited by what was coming out from the Council and relayed all this new 'people of God' theology directly to us. For years after that, I suffered because I didn't fit in. I arrived at the stage where I felt virtually on the outside of the Church, because everyone else seemed to be still talking the old language, while I was talking the new Vatican II language.

With a lot of my friends, I went to Queens University. I continued going to Mass, not through any sense of compulsion, but because I wanted to. I have always felt it was part of my life. At the same time, I was very much a free thinker and certainly didn't lead a particularly exemplary lifestyle. There was plenty of drinking at weekends and plenty of girl friends. Then I met Claire, and everything else became relative. We got married virtually immediately after we graduated from university, and started our family.

I was always drawn to the Church, in the belief that somehow being within the Church was keeping me within the grasp of God, but at no point along the way did I ever have the sense of having a personal relationship with God. Yet there was always a joy somehow. It was never a case of hanging in there because I was scared of hell or anything like that. I was far from being uncritical. I had come to see, for instance, that the Catholic Church was not the whole Church, but that the Church was the whole Body of Christ. At Mass on a Sunday, when I would recite in the Creed, 'I believe in the holy catholic church', I would deliberately qualify that as meaning the whole Body of Christ. After Vatican II's endorsement of personal conscience, it disturbed me to see the re-emergence of what seemed to be an overriding rigidity in the seventies. Nonetheless, I do believe that the Holy Spirit is really at work in the Catholic Church today through the ordinary people. In these days, God is awakening His people.

One day I read in the parish bulletin, 'If you want to complain about anything in the parish, why not come to the parish committee meeting?' So I went there to tell the priest a few things and before the end of the meeting, the Parish Priest announced, 'We would like to welcome the new member of our committee!' They ended up electing me chairman of the parish council!

Claire and I had taken a decision that we would not send our children to a Catholic school for their post-primary education. All my father's brothers went to the Protestant school in Ballycastle – there wasn't the same segregation in those days at all. So we sent the children to a well-known Belfast State grammar school, because it was a school that opened its doors to everybody without discrimination and we've always been very, very happy with the religious education that they received there. I was more than pleased that our daughter's religion teacher was a Presbyterian elder, who lived nearby and for whom we had great respect.

When our son was going on a school rugby tour last year, I went along to his religion teacher, who was going on the trip, and said, 'Will you look after my son on Sundays? If you're holding a Bible service or anything, I would ask you to involve him in it.' I was chiefly concerned that there would be some Christian aspect to what he was doing. I trusted my Protestant co-religionist to care for my son's spiritual welfare. My children received all their Scripture education from Church of Ireland or Presbyterian ministers who came into the school. My eldest daughter did have a bit of difficulty when she moved up from Bible Union to Scripture Union and some of the people there began to get a bit iffy about the possibility of Catholics being Christians. In the end, she stopped going.

Then, for her week of service on her way to the Duke of Edinburgh gold award, she decided to go on the Youth Team to Lourdes. We decided to take a holiday in France at the same time and left her off in Lourdes. I met an Irish group there, and was invited to join them at the grotto at twelve o'clock, to say the rosary, something I hadn't done for years. As it happened, I missed our rendezvous, but I could hear them in the background reciting the rosary. I remember sitting in front of the grotto in tears and making a promise that I would start to read the Scriptures again. When I came back home, I

got myself a Gideon Bible and started reading. I started
praying my way through the Bible, reading fifteen minutes of Scripture every day.

And then I saw an advert in the *Down and Connor
Herald* for a dioceasan course on evangelisation. I went
along and to my initial horror, found out that the course
would entail parish visitation, door-to-door work. My
first reaction was to get out of there quick, but I stayed
with it and for about twelve weeks we went through the
whole evangelisation process. This, of course, entailed an
evangelisation of oneself and so, right through, I faced an
awful lot of issues in my own life. And at the end of it all,
I was out and knocking on people's doors, telling them
about Jesus. I don't know at what precise point in the
course of those months I actually met Jesus in a personal
way. I know it was a struggle for me. It wasn't that I was
simply coming from being a pagan to being a Christian,
because I already was within the body of the Church. It
was rather a question of real discipleship. The Lord was
challenging me, 'Are you for Me or against Me? Are you
going to give up all this junk that's in your life?' There
were plenty of things that I had to really repent of. I had
also to contend with the devil's constant attempts to dis-
courage me with his belittling, ridiculing accusations.
But, eventually, I came across those wonderful words in
Romans 8:31–37, 'If God is for us, who can be against us?
. . . It is God who justifies . . . Who shall separate us from
the love of Christ? . . . we are more than conquerors
through him who loved us.' I held tightly on to those
verses and took them with me wherever I went. By the
end of that period, I certainly had come through a process to where I knew exactly who Jesus Christ was in my
life.

I still had this feeling of being somehow on the side-
lines of the Church. I always regarded myself as being
the least significant person in the group and always sat
quietly at the back. Then one day I was told about a new
four-week course on evangelisation that being held in

Rome. After much deliberation, I ended up taking a month off to go on one of these courses, the 'Paul' course, which was put together by a Catholic layman called Pepe Prado. It was a totally Scripture-centred course and it revolutionised my life. When I came back to the group, they were bowled over by the change they saw in me, at the new boldness and commitment the Lord had given me. During the course, when we were praying for a new release of the Holy Spirit in our lives to empower us for evangelism, I had asked for the gift of song. Now I suddenly found myself catapulted out of my customary back row position up to the front of the meeting to lead prayer and praise.

In the course of time, I have become very active in what is now known as the Siloam Community. Its focus is evangelisation. We meet at least once a week for prayer. We have gone out regularly in West Belfast, evangelising door to door, and have found that people are absolutely dying to hear about the Lord. We simply and unequivocally preach Jesus. From the moment we walk through the door we say that we're here to talk about God. I remember one particular man saying, 'Well, I'm not interested in that.' And we just said back to him, 'Look, we're not here to try and grab you and pull you down to the chapel on Sunday morning. We're here to tell you that God loves you.' On hearing that, he just said, 'Well, come on in.' If you're proclaiming the love of God and proclaiming Jesus, it just cuts through things like a hot knife through butter. And that's what we do when we're out visiting.

We now run the Paul course, which is designed to effectively teach Catholics the fundamentals of the plan of salvation and to equip them to give away this good news to others. Through the Word of God, people are brought to a full and clear personal knowledge of the Lord. I remember once, in the chaplaincy of the university where I lecture in engineering, a girl reciting the six-point plan she had learned on the course: God loves me.

I am a sinner. Jesus is my salvation. I must commit myself to Him and receive His Holy Spirit. I must get involved in Christian community. The Presbyterian chaplain sat there amazed at the realisation that the plan was substantially the same as that taught in the Scripture Union. It's really just a methodology of presenting the plan of salvation, which we use whenever we go out visiting door to door. The central point is that you need to recognise that you are a sinner and that Jesus is your salvation. It's got to be your personal decision.

Claire and I find ourselves increasingly building relationships with Christians from other Churches. We have come to appreciate the crucial importance of experiencing the interdenominational breadth of the Body of Christ. We are brothers and sisters in Christ and that's the long and the short of it. I have a friend, a Presbyterian elder, who calls for me every Saturday morning and we both go down to the Methodist prayer group. In my heart I am blessed by these folk and they tell me that my presence there as a Catholic is a great blessing to their group. For me, knowing Jesus personally has just knocked down barriers all over the place. We meet again later in the morning to pray for an hour together. Claire and I have also recently got involved with the Divine Healing Ministries in St Anne's Cathedral, in the belief that the Lord desires to perform signs and wonders to help people recognise the truth of the proclamation of Jesus Christ.

We recognise, when we evangelise people and encourage them to get involved in Christian community, that real Christian community does not exist in many parishes. But we know that we have to start with Christ first and then move towards community. You can't build community and then invite Christ in afterwards. Effectively, it's in the Lord's hands. We do know people who have started to gather their own little community groups. Also, some parishes are beginning to start cell groups. I'm convinced that the Lord will sort out the problem of how He will nurture those who have committed their lives to Him. Our primary task is to present people with the opportunity to do just that.

23

LIVING BY FAITH
REV PAT COLLINS C.M.

Pat Collins is a Vincentian priest. He lectures in spirituality in Dublin in both the Catholic Seminary and the Church of Ireland Seminary. He is a prominent conference speaker and author of a number of pamphlets and books.

I was born at the end of the war. My parents were devout Catholics. As a boy I was a regular churchgoer and always had the thought of becoming a priest. At the age of eighteen, I entered a seminary and was ordained in 1971. At that time my mind was full of theology and my heart full of good intentions. Within a year or so I was becoming disillusioned. While people sometimes commented favourably on my well-prepared sermons, I noticed that no one ever seemed to be changed by them. I also tried to help troubled people. I gave them good advice, but I began to realise that what was really needed was good news. I began to resent them, because, unconsciously, I saw my own emotional and spiritual poverty mirrored in theirs.

Baptism in the Spirit
I finally acknowledged this state of affairs as a result of reading an inspiring verse, Revelation 3:17: 'You say, "I am rich; I have acquired wealth and do not need a thing." But you do not realise that you are wretched, pitiful, poor, blind and naked.' From that moment onwards,

instead of identifying with the Good Samaritan as I had, I now identified with the man on the roadside. Like him, I felt wounded and weak. This acknowledgement of aching need became the birthplace of a heartfelt desire for a spiritual awakening. Over the next year and a half that yearning for a new experience of God deepened and strengthened. The Lord responded in the form of three providential events.

Firstly, on Easter Sunday 1973, I was invited to attend a charismatic prayer meeting in the Gregorian University in Rome. I was deeply impressed by the mutual affection of those attending, the sincerity of their testimonies and, most of all, by their singing in tongues, which sounded heavenly to me. I remember thinking, this is what I have been looking for, it is the Acts of the Apostles come alive.

Secondly, when I got home, I happened to buy a book entitled *Power in Praise* by Merlin Carothers. Among other things it described Baptism in the Spirit and encouraged readers to ask for this grace. This I did, many times.

Thirdly, in February 1974, I was invited to attend a Charismatic Conference in Benburb Priory in Co. Tyrone. On Saturday, February 4th, Rev Cecil Kerr, a Church of Ireland minister from the Christian Renewal Centre in Rostrevor, Co. Down, gave an inspiring talk about Jesus as our way of peace. Quite frankly, his anointed words moved me to tears. I wanted to know the Lord in the way that Cecil did. Afterwards a nun introduced me to him. We had a brief chat and arranged to meet privately. When we did, I told Cecil that I was looking for a new awareness of God in my life. Then he read the memorable passage from Ephesians 3:16–20 which asks that one '. . . may have power, together with all the saints, to grasp how wide and long and high and deep is the love of Christ, and to know this love that surpasses knowledge – that you may be filled to the measure of all the fullness of God'. Then he began to pray for me, first-

ly in English, then in tongues. Suddenly and effortlessly
I too began to pray fluently in tongues. I had been baptised in the Spirit.

For the next six months or so I was on a spiritual high;
inwardly I was flooded with a feeling of wellbeing. As
1 Peter 1:8 says, 'Though you have not seen him, you
love him and even though you do not see him now, you
believe in him and are filled with an inexpressible and
glorious joy.' I knew with great conviction that Jesus
loved me and accepted me as I was. It was as if He had
walked through the walls of my body to live within me
by His Spirit. There are some lines in a poem entitled
'True Love' by Sir Philip Sidney, which express something of what I felt.

> My true love hath my heart and I have his.
> His heart in me keeps him and me in one.
> My heart in him, his thoughts and senses guides.
> He loves my heart; for once it was his own.
> I cherish his, because in me it bides.

As a result of this new sense of the Divine indwelling, I
had a great love for Scripture. It was alive as never before
with spiritual meaning. Repeatedly the words leapt alive
off the page into my heart. Prayer was attractive and
easy. I even loved people more. My service of others,
especially by means of preaching and praying for people, was more effective.

Well, all that happened twenty-three years ago. Since
then I have come to a number of conclusions about
Baptism in the Spirit.

Firstly, as Montague and McDonnell have shown in
Christian Initiation and Baptism in the Spirit, from a
Catholic point of view, Baptism in the Spirit is integral to
the sacraments of initiation and normative for all
Christians.

Secondly, as Cardinal Suenen's first Malines
Document has suggested, whereas one received the Holy

Spirit in a sacramental way in baptism–confirmation, one received it in an experiential way as a result of Baptism in the Spirit.

Thirdly, as the Irish bishops have said in *Life in the Spirit*, Baptism in the Spirit is a conversion gift through which one receives a new and significant openness to the power and gifts of the Holy Spirit.

Fourthly, Baptism in the Spirit is merely the beginning of a new beginning. Rather than being a once-off event, it initiates an ongoing state or process.

Fifthly, St Thomas Aquinas argues in his *Summa Theologica* that this infilling by the Spirit can be deepened and strengthened by subsequent infillings (cf. Ephesians 5:18). He says that the Spirit dwells in a person in a new way in order that he or she may act in a new way. Rather than intensifying grace, such infillings extend its influence.

Be filled with the Spirit

Over the years, I have experienced many infillings of the Spirit that have deepened the state of my being baptised in the Spirit. In retrospect, I can see that most of them were connected with Eucharistic devotion. For example, a few years ago, a number of us were conducting a mission in the parish of the Holy Spirit in Dublin. I wasn't feeling well at the time. In retrospect I can see that I was suffering from emotional exhaustion. On one of the days – it happened to be my fortieth birthday – I was relieved to find that I hadn't been appointed to preach that night. However, at the eleventh hour, I was asked to be the celebrant at the Eucharist. I said, 'Yes', but experienced a profound feeling of powerlessness and emptiness. As I was vesting in the sacristy, I prayed, 'Lord, I am at the end of my tether. I am completely drained. I have nothing to offer. I am incapable of leading Your people in the celebration of the Eucharist. Unless You help me, my efforts will be in vain.'

With that, we proceeded to the sanctuary and the

Eucharist began. After a colleague had preached the
homily, I approached the altar to begin the offertory
prayers. Once again a feeling of powerlessness came
over me. I silently repeated the prayer I had said in the
sacristy and proceeded with the blessing of the gifts. As
I read the Eucharistic prayer, something strange happened. I became palpably aware of a mysterious
Presence. I was so moved emotionally by this realisation
that I couldn't speak for a few moments. During the
pause I was amazed to find that there was an uncanny
silence in the church. There wasn't a sound! No one was
coughing, moving or rustling paper. Evidently everyone
was aware of the Holy Presence. When I regained my
composure I said, 'I'm sure you can all sense it. The Holy
Spirit has come upon all of us, the Risen Lord is here.' As
I continued with the Eucharist, the sense of loving
Presence deepened. It was one of the most wonderful
experiences of my life.

   What a paradox! When I was at my lowest ebb, from
a human point of view, I was granted one of the greatest
blessings of my entire priestly ministry. Besides being
the best birthday present I ever received, it taught me
that, if we trust in God's goodness and love, we discover
that His grace is sufficient for us, for His power is made
perfect in weakness . . . for I can do all things through
Him who gives me strength (II Corinthians 12:9;
Philippians 4:13). Nowadays, when I am faced by similar
crucifixion points of powerlessness, I am increasingly
sustained by the conviction that the Lord blesses those
who put their trust in Him (Jeremiah 17:7). As a result, in
moments of need, I try to depend absolutely upon the
Lord. Let me give just one example of what I mean.

Living by faith
A few weeks ago, I flew to Canberra in Australia to
speak at a conference over the Pentecost weekend 1997.
On the way out, I noticed that I was getting a sore throat.
That worried me. I feared that it might cause me to have

many fits of coughing. After my arrival, I got a bad dose of laryngitis. My voice got weak and husky. By the time the conference began, speaking was quite a strain and by the Saturday afternoon, my voice had disappeared completely. When I opened my mouth not a single sound emerged. For the first time in my life I was utterly speechless and had to communicate in a whisper.

That night I found it hard to sleep. As Johann Wolfgang Von Goethe once wrote:

Who never ate his bread in sorrow
Who never spent the darksome hours
Weeping and watching for the morrow
He knows you not, you heavenly Power.

I decided to reflect and pray. I was mortified by the fact that I had come all this way, at great expense to my Australian hosts, and was unable to give all the scheduled talks. I poured out my feelings to the Lord. Then I recalled two verses from the Bible, which mean a lot to me. The first is Proverbs 3:5, 'Trust in the Lord with all your heart and lean not on your own understanding', and the second is Psalm 37:5 which says, 'Commit your way to the Lord; trust in him and he will act.' Then I said, 'Heavenly Father, I have travelled thousands of miles in order to preach Your Word. Now that I have no voice, I am anxious and embarrassed. But I believe in Your plan and provision for my life. Trusting in Your promise in Isaiah 41:10, I will not be afraid. I entrust this whole situation to You. I ask You to restore my voice, at least enough to be able to communicate with the help of the sound system. I cast all my anxieties upon You in the confident belief that You care about me and I thank You that You hear my prayer.' I had a real sense of the presence, goodness and trustworthiness of the Lord and was convinced that He would help me in my hour of need.

When I got up in the morning, I took a shower and tried to speak, but not a sound could I make. When it was obvious at breakfast that I was as dumb as Zechariah was, a priest companion said he would give a substitute talk. After the meal was over I went to my room. I had a subjective conviction that, despite all indications to the contrary, God would answer my prayers. So I went to the priest who had offered to speak in my stead and said in a whisper, 'When it's time for the talk, I'd like to step forward to the microphone and try to speak. If I can't, you take over.' He agreed. When we got to the conference venue, there was prayer and praise for about forty minutes. Then I stepped forward to the microphone. I felt like St Peter stepping out of the boat to walk on water. My chosen subject happened to be, 'Trusting in divine providence'. I opened my lips, trusted in God and, wonder of wonders, I could speak. True, my voice was weak and husky, but I could speak and the amplification compensated for my lack of volume. It was a very emotional moment for me. God, my loving and ever-faithful Father, had heard my prayer. He had literally given me the gift of tongues. In the event I gave a fifty-minute talk, preached a homily at the Eucharist and later on conducted a healing service. Since then, the organisers have written to say that they have 'heard testimonies of physical healings as well as "miraculous" reconciliations'.

Conclusion

Writing in 1979, Pope John Paul II described the role of the Holy Spirit in these words:

> Only the Spirit enables us to say to God, 'Abba Father'. Without the Spirit we cannot say, 'Jesus is Lord'. From the Spirit come all the charisms that build up the church, the community of Christians. In keeping with this, St Paul gives each disciple of Christ the instruction: 'Be filled with the Spirit'.

Believing this to be true, I say the following prayer each

morning, for the infilling and guidance of the Holy Spirit.

Father in heaven, Your Spirit is a Spirit of truth and love. Pour that same Holy Spirit into my body, my mind and my soul! Preserve me this day from all illusions and false inspirations. Reveal Your presence and Your Word to me in a way that I can understand and I thank You that You will do this, while giving me the ability to respond, through Jesus Christ our Lord. Amen.

24

FREEDOM FROM DEPRESSION
JOE DALTON

Joe is a full-time Catholic lay missionary with an international ministry, who lives near Dun Laoghaire. He has a powerful testimony of being healed from thirty-one years of chronic depression. He has a dynamic healing ministry, leads retreats, conferences and Life in the Spirit seminars.

For thirty-one years I suffered from constant depression. I think it was brought on by my feeling always in the shadow of my father, a tough policeman, who hit first and asked questions afterwards! I constantly felt the need to prove myself. Religion, too, played its part. Brought up in a Catholic school in Limerick, I was taught all the rules but told nothing about the enabling power of a living relationship with Jesus Christ. I found myself constantly falling short of the high standards set for me. Never quite at peace with my conscience, I existed rather than lived.

When I was twelve years of age I was molested in a cinema, before I even knew the facts of life. When I went to confess my sins to the priest, he told me I was a disgrace to my family and nearly threw me out of the confessional. That was my introduction to the tender loving mercies of Jesus. A terrible depression set in from that time. I felt defiled, unclean and unforgiven. I wanted to kill myself because I felt that every day I was offending God and that I could not live up to the standards that God had written on my heart. At one stage it got so bad I was praying to die.

When I was seventeen, my father, who had left the police and started a truck business, was forced into bankruptcy. He started to drink very heavily. He was drinking two bottles of whiskey a day and smoking a hundred cigarettes and my mother was crying most of the time. I had planned to join the army as an officer cadet, but now had to stay at home and find work. For twelve years I handed over my pay packet, unopened, to my mother. I lived daily in the belief that, as far as my life was concerned, God had dealt me a bad hand.

I used to play a lot of sport – hurling, football and rowing. Then one day some fellow heard me singing and told me I should do something about my voice. I didn't know whether he meant that I was afflicting his ears, or that I should have my voice trained! I studied music for several years in Dublin at the Royal Irish Academy, and subsequently in the University of Vienna. I won the gold medal singing at the National Festival. I went on to win ten other major awards, singing with the Dublin Grand Opera Society and the Irish State Opera, singing oratorio and musical comedy, doing broadcasts, recitals and cabaret – and getting my name in the International *Who's Who*. But I was still miserable. Outward success and inner despair.

I married Pat, a very beautiful Limerick girl. At one stage, we had five children under six, three of them under eighteen months! I was often away from home, but never once heard her complain. Eventually I collapsed under my heavy schedule and was hospitalised. On the doctor's advice, I began seeing a psychiatrist for treatment for my depression, but all he had to offer me was librium and valium. The depression was so black that I just wanted to kill myself. For a period of six months, I got down on my knees every night and begged God to forgive me and to take me in my sleep. But each morning I found myself awaking to face yet another day.

I would go out on stage and sing at concerts and sometimes get a standing ovation and then I'd come home and weep, because of the terrible emptiness inside me. Blaise Pascal, a French theologian, said that there is a God-shaped void in every human heart. Only Christ can fill it. Augustine said, 'We were made for Thee, O Lord, and our hearts will never rest until they find their rest in Thee.'

About a year later, on the commuter train to work, I felt drawn to speak to a man who always looked so happy that he had really begun to irritate me. It transpired that he attributed his happiness to his involvement in what he called 'Charismatic Renewal'. I retorted that if he, like me, had a job in the Civil Service – especially in its Post Office Telephone Department – and a mortgage, and a wife and five kids, then maybe he would be miserable too! He burst out laughing and replied: 'It just so happens that I have a job in the Civil Service, in the Post Office Telephone Department, and a mortgage, and a wife and five kids. In fact, I work in the same building as you!'

He then gave me a book called *Prison to Praise*, by Merlin Carothers. There I read that, no matter how hard you try, you can't save yourself. Christ is the only one who can do the saving. He can pull anyone out of the pit who will put their hand in His. All that is required is to tell God you're sorry for your sins. Tell Him you can't save yourself and that you acknowledge Him as your Saviour. Invite Him into your life and ask Him to change you to be the person He wants you to be. Then ask Him to release His Holy Spirit within you. It's that simple.

So I got down on my knees in the dark in my room one night and cried out to God and said, 'Lord, You know I've been trying and miserably failing. You are my Saviour, so I'm asking You to come into my heart and to change me to the way You want me to be. Take from me anything You need to take – my wife, my children, the house, the job, the music, anything. I will never complain again. Just change me to be the way You want me to be. If there is this power of Your Holy Spirit, which will help me to do the will of the Father and help me to succeed where I have failed before, may I have that too and I will praise You with my dying breath.' Immediately the whole room was filled with the glory of God. It was like a cloud of intensely bright light, which filled the room. It totally enveloped me and penetrated every fibre of my being. I felt myself caught up in it, caressed in the love of Christ, and in one instant my depression was gone and I knew it would never return. All the fear, worry, guilt, scruples and doubt were wiped out. Until then I had been a foul-mouthed individual – that was no more. I was ready to walk straight into heaven.

Twelve years ago I decided to quit my job, and quit the singing and everything else and to work on a full-time basis for the Lord. I have been doing that ever since. I have been His witness in Jerusalem and in Judea and Samaria and all over the place. I have seen people healed of most diseases. God has been providing for Pat, myself and our family. We've never wanted for anything and have never had to ask anyone for one penny. And I really would not swap places with anyone on earth for all the money in the world. Praise God!

As a Catholic, I find my relationship with the Lord nourished and deepened day by day. I believe that when we eat the flesh of the Son of Man and drink His blood, we have eternal life and He will raise us up at the last day. So that has become a priority for me, to receive the Eucharist every day of my life. But as well as that, to read Scripture, which is more important to me than anything else. I stand on the Word of God. We live by the Word of God – Christ is as truly present in the Word as He is in the Eucharist. Prayer and fasting are also very important in my life. I have been fasting a couple of days a week for twenty-two years now.

God is doing a mighty thing in this land. I've seen thousands and thousands of people come to Life in the Spirit seminars all over Ireland, where I've had the privilege of sharing the Good News with them and then leading them to commit their lives to Jesus. Many have been baptised in the Holy Spirit and many have been healed. In Longford, for example, 2,000 people attended the seminars. At Kilnacrot Abbey in Cavan 1,100 attended. And so it has been all over Ireland, north, south, east and west. I believe there's a great hunger for the Word of God in this country. I also believe that the Lord is building His Church here, as He said, 'I will build my church'. He has determined to do it.

I owe so much to Christians of other denominations. I wouldn't be as I am without them. I am so greatly indebted to the Methodist minister, Merlin Carothers, for his book *Prison to Praise*. I wouldn't have known about the Full Gospel Businessmen's Fellowship, without Presbyterians, Baptists and Methodists from that Fellowship coming down from the North of Ireland and telling us the Good News. I wouldn't have known about fasting had I not learned about it from the Pentecostals Jack and Patty Chapple. I wouldn't have been aware of the power of the Eucharist to heal if I hadn't seen a video of a satellite link between Anaheim in California and Seoul in South Korea, where a Pentecostal speaker said, 'You know, I believe this to be part of the body of Christ and when I eat of this, I'm totally, physically healed. And when I drink of the cup, every sin that I've ever committed, for which I've repented and confessed, is wiped away. I receive total healing of spirit, mind, body and emotions.' It was that which led me to a new and deeper realisation of what can happen in the Eucharist when we receive it, discerning the Body of the Lord. None of these were Catholic and yet they so deeply touched and influenced my life. I have been fed by the books they have written. I have benefitted from their great insight into the Word of God, from their teachings on subjects such as healing and deliverance, for example. I have learned so much from them on so many topics which I have never heard expounded in our own Church. I thank God for them. They are my brothers and sisters in Christ.

25

A New Pentecost in Ireland

Larry Kelly

Larry leads the Lamb of God Community in North Belfast and has been a pioneer in interdenominational relationships in Belfast over the past 20 years. A trustee of the Christian Renewal Centre in Rostrevor, Larry leads cross-denominational Alpha Bible Study Courses in Belfast.

I was born in 1934 in the County Down parish of Dundrum, into a family of ten children: six boys and four girls. I barely remember my father, who died when I was very young. My mother had the responsibility of rearing the ten of us. She was a woman of great faith, much prayer and strong spirit. My faith was nourished by her example. Growing up in this traditional Catholic family, I saw myself as a faithful, committed member of the Catholic Church. I suppose one of the big difficulties I experienced in my early teenage years was the move from life in the country to life in Belfast. I was a rather shy young fellow and found it really difficult to settle into my new surroundings and my new school.

On leaving school, I joined the Civil Service as a clerical officer in the Customs and Excise Department in London. This again took a lot of adjusting for me. After about two and a half years in London (in the early fifties), I found myself due to register for the two years compulsory National Service in the Forces. I had already joined a part-time branch of The Royal Marine Volunteer Reserves, which offered a good deal of opportunity for fun, excitement and adventure at weekends. I was therefore very keen to go into National Service, which had taken many of my friends all over the world, to Africa, the Middle East, Korea etc. But back home in Belfast, my mother had other ideas. She launched fervently into a novena (nine days of prayers), praying that I would not have to do National Service. Totally unexpectedly, I got called up to our Personnel Department and was asked if I would like to go back to Belfast on a temporary transfer. Northern Ireland residents were exempt from National Service. I reluctantly agreed and, within a short time, was offered a permanent post in Belfast. My mother's prayers were answered!

For a time, I was part of the crowd, drinking and partying at weekends, doing all the mandatory things that were supposed to constitute 'a good time'. But I was left unsatisfied, unhappy in myself. There was a loneliness in me, a spiritual hunger for something more substantial in life. I was still a very committed member of the Church. This was pre-Vatican II, when we believed that the Catholic Church was the one true Church, all others being outside. I joined the Clonard Men's Confraternity, which was a very strong confraternity of around ten thousand men, who met three times a week in the church for prayer and very good teaching from the Redemptorist Fathers, based in the Clonard Monastery in West Belfast. Then, in 1959, I was asked to join the Legion of Mary, which was very involved in all sorts of social work. They ran hostels for the destitute, for prostitutes and for unmarried mothers. They were also involved in evangelisation – street work and door-to-door work. It was a tremendous challenge for me and had a very significant effect on my spiritual life. It had a very strict code of practice, requiring a commitment to a few hours active work each week and attendance at weekly meetings for prayer, discussion on spiritual topics and reporting on the work done. The work in our particular branch entailed going into Belfast at night, starting at about 9 p.m., to approach men who hung about some of the

worst areas of the city and talk to them about God. I
stuck with it and it helped me greatly in building up my
own personality and character and in overcoming a lot of
fear. In time, I became president of that group, and continued there for a number of years. Interestingly, despite
its title, it was the Holy Spirit who was the Patron of the
Legion of Mary. This is probably little understood, even
by some of the members. It was the Holy Spirit who was
to be looked to, rather than Mary. She was to be regarded as the model of one who was most open to the Spirit.

In the early sixties, I met a girl, Mary, and in 1963 we
got married. Then in 1971, a friend of mine, Frank Forte,
a very devout Catholic, asked me to read 1 Corinthians
chapters 12, 13 and 14, all about charismatic activity in
the early Church. It made no impression on me. He then
began to witness about what had happened to him. He
had some Pentecostal friends and, as was the usual practice in those days, had had many discussions and strong
arguments with them about the weaknesses of their relative churches. At some point they'd come to an understanding that this wasn't getting them anywhere, so
they'd begun to pray together. Following that, Frank had
experienced the 'Baptism of the Spirit'. I had read about
such strange goings-on among Catholics in America –
people getting over-enthusiastic about their religion,
waving their hands in the air, praying in tongues and
experiencing all sorts of strange phenomena which were
outside normal Catholic experience.

Eventually I agreed to go to a meeting where I heard
a Dominican priest describe what was happening in the
Church as 'a new Pentecost . . . Catholic Pentecostalism'.
I was greatly impressed. At a further meeting, as we sat
in prayer together, I really became aware, for the first
time, of the truth of that Scripture, 'Where two or three
are gathered together in my name, there am I in the
midst.' I really sensed the Lord's presence that night. We
started a little prayer group of our own, all devoted
Catholics and members of the Legion of Mary. Then

Frank joined us and introduced the charismatic dimension into the group which, initially, caused a bit of tension. Frank had his name registered in America as a contact person in Northern Ireland for Catholic Charismatic Renewal, or Catholic Pentecostalism as it was known at that time. So people arriving in from the States would contact Frank and he would often invite them to give an input at our meeting. Priests and nuns, whom we tended to listen to more seriously than to lay people, inundated us with stories of the work of the Spirit amongst Catholics in America.

I came to the point where I realised there was more to the Christian life than I had ever imagined. but I was still quite fearful about the implications of it all. I kept putting off making a decision about offering myself for prayer for Baptism in the Holy Spirit. Then one night I plucked up the courage and asked Frank to pray with me. I had a very powerful experience of the power of the love of God flowing through me. A great change took place within me and that transformation has continued. I have come to know something of what Paul meant when he said, 'We are being changed from one degree of glory to another, even as by the Spirit of the Lord'. I went home that night on cloud nine. I just felt this new life in me – I was elated. I knew something very important had happened to me, but I had no words to begin to describe it. It took me two or three weeks before I attempted to tell Mary about it. She immediately told me that she had noticed the change in me, that I wasn't as difficult to live with! So I thought, 'Well, if my wife notices a change in me, then this has got to be real!' After a time, Mary said she'd like to be baptised in the Spirit as well and asked if I would pray with her. I said, 'No, but I can get you someone who will.' She said that she didn't want anyone else, she only wanted me to pray with her. I tried to convince her that it would be better to get someone else, but she was adamant. So I eventually plucked up the courage and prayed with her and she too had an experi-

ence of the Baptism of the Spirit that night. I had been of
the opinion that God could use anybody else, but not me.
God taught me the lesson, through my wife, that He can
use any of us, if we're open to Him.

Things began to happen from then on. First of all, we
had a family of four young children and found that we
needed to extend our accommodation. I had to take off
time from my involvement with the Legion of Mary to
get this work under way. At the same time, the prayer
group was growing considerably in numbers, as was our
involvement with Protestant organisations. This was one
of the great highlights in my life at that time, finding
Protestants coming in to the prayer group and discovering that we could live together, pray together and find a
unity together. It was so exciting. We have such a need
here in Northern Ireland for this shared experience of the
Spirit. At any rate, by the time the house was completed,
I just wasn't in a position to take up the Legion of Mary
work again, due to other pressures. Not only was our
own prayer group growing, but other prayer groups
were asking me to come and talk about the work of the
Holy Spirit. It was an exciting time, full of hope.
Presbyterians, Methodists and especially Pentecostals
were coming along to our meetings.

Then I had the privilege of going to a National
Catholic Conference in Notre Dame University in
America. It was a really impressive experience, with
something like 30,000 people attending, including over
1,000 clergy, and attracting a visit from Cardinal
Suenens. We began to realise that this movement was of
great significance for the Church. Some time after that,
we had the first International Catholic Charismatic
Conference in Rome. The leaders met with the Pope,
who said that he saw this Renewal Movement as a
chance for the Church and for the world. This greatly
encouraged us. We saw the work of the Holy Spirit as
Vatican II bearing fruit in the life of the Church. A new
Pentecost had begun and we were in the forefront of

it in Ireland.

I was part of a core group of ten looking after what had become a very large interdenominational prayer group, a very new experience for all of us. We also felt a responsibility for the oversight of other prayer groups. We decided to form a community where we would be able to share our faith more deeply and be a greater support to one another. So in 1977 we formed what we called The Lamb of God Community, conscious of the suffering of the people around us and inspired with the conviction that praise of God was to be a priority for us. Trusting the Lord to bring in the money, we purchased premises in Duncairn Gardens, where we could be a presence for peace in an area of conflict. I resigned from the Civil Service to work full-time for the community.

We are currently involved in a number of ecumenical and cross-community initiatives. We participate in the Lower Antrim Road Clergy Fellowship, which regularly brings together priests and ministers from this area. Once a year, we sponsor a Week of Mission, with speakers such as Fr. Jim Burke and Rev Cecil Kerr, which alternates between Presbyterian, Church of Ireland and Roman Catholic churches.

Our base is now in Shalom House, at 12 Cliftonville Road in North Belfast. Various cross-community activities are run from here – Basic Adult Education Programme, Alcoholics Anonymous, Therapeutic Creche for Single Parents (referred from Social Services Board), Scripture Study, Prayer Meeting and a Prayer and Counselling Ministry. We have recently launched a 'Bridging the Gap' educational programme, facilitated by Sr. Cecelia Clegg and Dr Joe Leichty (a Menonite). We also run a daily Drop-In Centre. People who suffer from mental illnesses, such as schizophrenia, call in for a cup of tea and a chat. We co-ordinate the activities of twenty volunteers, who visit the elderly in the community. We have also had the pleasure of joining with the Christian Fellowship Church, one of the New Churches, in running a 'Better Understanding' programme.

Ministry Teams go out from The Lamb of God Community, promoting Christ-centred, biblically-based renewal in various Catholic parishes. For example, in Carrickfergus, we are currently assisting a Life in the Spirit seminar, which is being attended by seventy people, including the parish priest. Overall, I believe, we are a praying presence in North Belfast, out of which new hope is springing up.

Looking back over my life, I can only marvel at God's faithfulness to me, at how patient and gentle He has been in drawing me by His Holy Spirit into an ever-deeper knowledge of Himself and into a fuller commitment to His service.

26

MY ADVENTURE FOR PEACE

ANGELA MCANESPIE

Angela is a school teacher from County Tyrone, who is involved in interdenominational community work.

I was born and brought up in a traditional Catholic family. I had an awareness of God, was reasonably faithful to daily prayers and attended Mass regularly. I was comfortable with my faith, and through school and teacher training college led a relatively untroubled life, graduating as a primary school teacher and taking up a post in a school in Moy, Co. Armagh.

Then at the age of thirty-three, I had a riding accident and injured my back. As I lay in traction in hospital, I turned to prayer in a wholehearted way. As the psalmist says, *'Out of the depths I cry to Thee, O Lord.'* The specialist, Mr McCloud, came to see me and suggested transferring me to Musgrave Park Hospital in Belfast for an operation. The sister in charge of the ward advised me not to be in a hurry to have back surgery as there was only a fifty per cent chance of success and I could be left completely paralysed. I took her advice and left hospital, still suffering great pain.

I continued storming heaven, asking the Holy Spirit to give me help. Then one night, when I was praying in bed, I experienced a tremendous outpouring of God's love. It was as if my whole body was filled to overflowing. Jesus became intensely real, as if He had walked through the walls of my body to live within me. This experience opened up for me a whole new intimacy in prayer. I felt so much joy that sentiments of praise, glory, thanksgiving and adoration began to flow spontaneously from my heart. The Scriptures had new meaning and force and I read everything I could lay my hands on to satisfy the hunger I had for the Word of God.

I did not know how to begin to share my experience with anyone else. In a way, it was so precious to me I didn't want to share it, in case people, through lack of understanding, might belittle it. But there was no hiding the change in me, and people noticed! Before this I had always found teaching religion very difficult and felt very inadequate to the task. I had been particularly irritable with the children the previous week, because of the pain in my back. But now, as I went into my class and surveyed them, I felt I wanted to hug them individually, they appeared so precious to me. I experienced a strong sensation of real joy as I opened the Religion textbook and prepared to teach. Now there was Someone I really wanted to talk about! I really felt I was getting help in my teaching, and there was a much greater response from the children. Results that term were better than ever before.

When I entered the staff-room, I had the same experience of love and compassion for the people there. I saw them, as never before, as unique individuals, each with their own set of problems, and I experienced a deep desire for their personal happiness, a desire to do what I could to bring that about.

Then I discovered that the fears and anxieties that had previously plagued me were completely gone. I had been full of fears – fear of death, fear of walking past the graveyard, fear of the dark, fear of being in the house alone – it was a long list! When my mother had to spend a time in hospital, leaving me alone in the house, I was terrified. At night, I had to leave every light in the house on. I was so afraid I couldn't get to sleep. Now I was able to put all the lights off, go to bed and sleep in peace. The difference was that I knew I was no longer alone. I had such an awareness of how close God was to me. I really knew, experientially, that 'in Him we live and move and have our being'. There was a wholly new joy in my life. Prayer was a delight. When I went to Mass, it was as if I was hearing the prayers for the first time. They were now charged with meaning. I felt I wanted to repeat them.

About six months after this, a friend invited me to a 'charismatic' prayer group in nearby Benburb. I went along somewhat hesitantly, only to discover there a whole group of people who had experienced the reality of God in a similar way to myself. I felt totally at home among people who wanted to praise and worship God openly. It was such a joy for me to be able, at last, to publicly and freely praise God in the uninhibited way in which I felt He deserved to be praised. At the meeting, I met a man called Des Heaney from Lurgan, who told me about his dramatic healing. His hip was shattered in a shooting incident in Belfast and he had had great difficulty getting about on crutches and needed constant help. Then he went to a healing service in Benburb and, within half an hour, he was completely cured. As an added bonus, he was also cured of a drinking problem.

Des' testimony built up my faith. I'd had a particularly bad day in school. The pain in my back caused me to be irritable with the children. When I was praying that night, I thought, 'This can't be God's will. I would be able to do my work better and be more loving to the children and serve Him better if my back was healed.' I then put my two hands on my back and asked God to heal it. In my imagination I saw the light of God shining up and down my spine, healing it. Time seemed to stand still and I felt a great awareness of God's presence and peace. The following morning my first realisation on waking was, 'My back is better!' I jumped out of bed without a twinge. I was called back to the hospital for a check-up two weeks later and the new X-rays confirmed that my back was completely healed.

Like many people who have been healed themselves, I had the desire and the faith conviction to pray for others. Happily, over the years, I've seen men and women recovering from physical and psychological illnesses. Experience convinces me that Jesus of Nazareth continues His healing ministry through members of the Christian community (cf. Mark 16:17–18).

September 1976 was another crossroads in my life. During the National Conference on Charismatic Renewal, the Rev David Watson spoke about how blessed the peacemakers were in God's eyes. It seemed he threw a challenge directly to me when he quoted these words: 'Happy are those who dream dreams and are willing to pay the price to make their dreams come true.'

My dream was of peace in Northern Ireland, but what could I do? I lived in what was infamously known as the Murder Triangle, so many people had been killed by paramilitaries. Four of the children in my class had had their fathers murdered. Two brothers from a local Protestant family were murdered one morning quite close to the school. Feelings ran very deep and bitter in that area. I witnessed such awful pain in Protestant and Catholic homes alike, I longed to be able to do something to help end the heartache.

For a whole week I prayed for guidance. I implored God to show me what to do, because I didn't know how to get involved. His reply took me by surprise. The following Saturday, I attended a small local Peace Rally. Before the afternoon was over, I had been asked to organise the major rally at which Betty Williams, one of the winners of the Nobel Peace Prize, was going to speak. With David Watson's words ringing in my ears, I realised that the Lord was giving me the direction I had prayed for. I accepted. Two weeks later, more than 20,000 came to Dungannon. They came in busloads from all over the North to an area scarred by violence, fear and murder. Protestant Shankill and Catholic Falls, they held hands and sang, 'Abide With Me'. More rallies were held and similar scenes were enacted as we joined hands to sing and pray for peace.

But many of us realised that rallies alone weren't enough to bring about the changes we wanted to see. More was needed. A conference was convened by the different organisations for peace in the North, called 'Waging Peace'. As we sat together working out our future strategy, we saw how much effort, hard work and sacrifice was going to be required. The wound to be healed had been festering for centuries. Someone once said of us in Northern Ireland, 'We are a race apart'. We live apart, we work apart, we pray apart, we have never learned to come together, nor made an attempt, because there are no institutions that make it possible. What was needed were bridges across which people from different communities could communicate. We knew ways would have to be worked out that would bring Protestants and Catholics together, now that the rallies were over.

All this time I continued to attend interdenominational prayer meetings. I felt so strongly now that Protestants and Catholics were brothers and sisters in Christ. I knew the Lord was saying that He wanted us to come together, it was His will. Reconciliation became a priority for me. I felt, and continue to feel, that if we as Christians are not involved in God's movement of reconciliation, we are going against the Holy Spirit. In interdenominational gatherings, such as the Christian Renewal Centre in Rostrevor, other Christians provided me with the inspiration and the spiritual strength I needed. Inspired by 2 Corinthians 5:18–21, which speaks of the ministry of reconciliation given us by Christ, I began to employ all of my spare time in peace activities.

I joined with others to organise Youth Camps in Norway for Protestant and Catholic teenagers, to enable them to get to know one another in a neutral environment. After one such camp, two sixteen-year-old girls, one Catholic, one Protestant, called at my home. They told me they had travelled to school in Dungannon on the same bus for five years, and had never once spoken to each other. Now they had become friends.

As a teacher, I was already involved in the Teachers' Union and its committees. I was able to get teachers to think about ways of building practical bridges of communication between Protestants and Catholics in the schools. I also felt a great need for a Peace Programme, which would begin in the primary schools, and started to pray in earnest about this. I really felt God wanted something done in this area, starting with children at an early, impressionable age. Then one day, out of the blue, I had a telephone call from Rev John Knox, who was Chairman of the Irish Council of Churches. He said they had come together with the Irish Commission for Justice and Peace to sponsor a Peace Education Programme for Schools, and asked me if I would be interested in working on it. This resulted in a programme called 'Free to be', one of the aims of which was to help the children to respect the dignity of every human being, no matter what their colour, class, religion or nationality. The programme was launched simultaneously in Belfast and Dublin. I was delighted when the Department of Education in Northern Ireland took it on board and sent out literature to all its schools to encourage them to use it.

I work on for reconciliation here in Northern Ireland. It is of paramount importance to me, because I believe that it is of paramount importance to my Lord. My conviction is that Christ is the keystone in any bridge for peace. He is our Peace. I see Him breaking down the dividing walls between Protestants and Catholics and making them one in His Name. My adventure for peace continues.

27

THE 'PROD' THAT LED ME TO GOD

PETER MCCANN

Peter is Director of The Well, a thriving YMCA drop-in centre in Lurgan, Co. Armagh, open to both Catholic and Protestant young people.

I come from a big Catholic family of twelve kids. I was about the middle, fifth down. My father was a businessman, a real entrepreneur. At Christmas time, he would rope us all in to help him make artificial Christmas trees. He would try his hand at anything and he had a rare way with words. He'd charm the birds out of the sky. He wasn't what you might call very religious, but he was a good man, loving and caring. I wasn't really religious either, though at school I used to think I'd like to become a Brother, mainly because I wanted to teach. I had a kind of faith and I always went to Mass. It was handed down to me mainly through my mother. 'Your da,' she'd say, 'is different.'

I was very good at sports, especially football. At the age of eighteen, I was invited over to Glasgow to try out for Celtic. Jock Stein wanted to sign me up, but I hated Glasgow and wouldn't stay. Two years later, they won the European Cup and I was kicking myself at the thought that I could have been part of it! I had football in my blood. I was good and I knew it. I had what was known as a Mohammed Ali complex. Everywhere I

went, I brought a pair of boots with me. I would be
offered jobs on the strength of my football skills. I was
given a job in British Airways in London so they could
have me on their team. And it was the same for many
other jobs, because I never stayed long in any one place.
Like my father, I would turn my hand to anything.

Patti and I married young. We had been sort of childhood sweethearts. It wasn't easy for her, with me running back and forth to England all the time. I never had
anything solid in my life. Then Patti became pregnant
and I decided that joining the British Air Force would
bring some stability into my life. That was just before the
Troubles began, around 1968. Again, my football boots
opened the way for me; I was made a corporal within a
year. I really enjoyed my time in the Air Force, but the
Troubles put an end to it. It wasn't safe for me to go
home to Belfast. My family were ostracised because I
was regarded as a traitor. The last straw came when a
brick was hurled through a window in my mother's
house. I had to resign.

This led to a very dark period in my life, twelve years
of wheeling and dealing and living in the fast lane.
Money went through my hands like water. I finally
reached the depths of despair. My marriage was on the
brink of collapse. I ended up one day, penniless and job-
less at forty years of age, standing thumbing a lift to
Dublin on Kennedy Road, near the M1. That was a dan-
gerous thing to do in those days, since there had been a
lot of random sectarian murders in that particular area of
Belfast, but I didn't care. I was in such a low state that I
would have welcomed a bullet to end it all. I remember
crying out to God and saying that if He would send me
someone who could get me out of the mess I was in, I
would turn my life over to Him. A car slowed down and
stopped a little way ahead. The driver was a thickset
man and he had a woman passenger beside him. She got
into the back seat and I sat in beside the driver. His shirt
sleeves were rolled up and his arms were covered in

UVF tatoos. As he drove off, I thought, 'This is it. The woman will shoot me in the back of the head and I'll be dumped at the side of the M1, another statistic.'

The man told me an amazing story, though I must confess I found it hard to give my whole attention to what he was saying. I kept waiting to feel the gun barrel in the back of my neck. He said his name was Packy Hamilton. He had been imprisoned for his activities as a member of the Ulster Volunteer Force, but while he was in prison he had come to know Jesus Christ and his whole life had been turned around. He spent all his time now telling people, especially his former paramilitary comrades, about the new life that Jesus offered. He often spoke at meetings together with an ex-INLA man who had also given his life to Jesus while in prison. I played along as best I could and then, at Newry, he said, 'We're branching off here to go to a meeting in Rostrevor. Would you like to come?' No, thanks, I had urgent business in Dublin. 'Do you mind if I just say a prayer with you?' I bowed my head but tried my best, without being too obvious, to keep my eye on both of them. Was this going to the point of delivery, my last moment?

I don't remember exactly what Packy prayed. I know my heart broke and I gave my life to Jesus Christ. I got out of the car a changed man and headed back to my wife in Belfast. She was overwhelmed at what had happened to me, after all her years of praying for me. I have no doubt of the strong connection between Patti's faithful prayers and the answer God sent that day by the side of the road. And what an answer! A Prod had led me to God! Not a priest or a nun, but an ex-UVF gunman! All my wonderful, fantastic, brilliant manoeuvring, all my skill, had left me sunk in a pit of sin and self-loathing, and God sent one of the people I would have most despised on earth to point me to the way out, Jesus.

I had such hunger for God. I didn't want the easy way, I wanted to convert Russia right away. I was on fire for Jesus. I'm telling you, sparks flew. I was organising this, I was organising that. I wanted prayer groups set up here and there. If somebody needed something, I'd be there. I used to go back to Packy's place – he was part of Prison Fellowship. I made contacts with all the heavies, all the UVF men and their families. I ended up working for Prison Fellowship for about a year, doing a lot of travelling. That was tremendous training for me. It slowed me down a bit. God has a wonderful way with Him. He had quite a job to do on me. There I was, firing on all cylinders, all you could see were scorch marks behind me, for God. I'd say, Hang on, what do you want me to do, Lord? Do you want me to build a temple in the middle of Belfast? I'd have done anything.

When I look back, it was wonderful. I think I'd call it the honeymoon period, though it lasted about seven or eight years! I felt I had got to let these people know about Jesus Christ and His love. Then He started teaching me about His purposes – about what He wanted and not what Peter McCann wanted. There was too much of me in all that I was doing. Somebody told me one day that, as he had been praying for me, he saw me running ahead of the Lord and the Lord holding on to my belt and laughing! I thought that was fabulous. It was true, of course. With me, it was a case of, 'I'm off, Lord! You hang on, I know the way!' There were times when I tried to do my own thing again, but the Lord reined me in each time. He rebukes those He loves. Bit by bit, He started to mould me and allow things into my life which slowed me down. Gently, so gently, He started to teach me and to train me in His ways. I wouldn't listen to anybody else, so only He, by His Holy Spirit, could teach me. And as He taught, He blessed. He blessed me in my family and He blessed me in my wife, in the deepening love between us.

We had eight kids, four boys and four girls, and we lived for nine years in a tough area in Lurgan. Sometimes it was very hard. There were times when I couldn't get any work and money was scarce. But God would always be there for us. He would be in there, providing for every need. He constantly encouraged us by letting us know, in the many simple, direct ways in which He answered our prayers, just how attentive He was to us. I'm so grateful as I look back at all He did for me, and what He's still doing for me, every day. In all that time, probably the biggest lesson the Lord taught me was that I had to get my own home in order before I could do anything else for Him. I wanted to work with everybody else, but I had to start in my own family. He showed me that my wife and children were my first prayer group, my first responsibility. One of my sons is a teacher. I have a daughter who is a doctor and two are nurses. Dominic is going to be an outdoor pursuits instructor, and Ronan is going to be a lawyer. Peter's a professional footballer; he's going to be playing for Blackburn Rovers – he's already signed for them. And then there's Rachel, the baby. And through all these years I've had a wife who supported me through thick and thin, a wonderful, blessed woman, with tremendous wisdom that God has blessed her with. She's a qualified nurse and is now a trained counsellor – she's had plenty of experience, with all that she had to go through with me! It's a miracle she hung on to me at all. But now we both love Jesus, we live life for Him.

The Lord had let me know that He had a work already prepared for me and that I was to get my act together and wait for it to come. So I learned as I waited on the Lord. Then one day, three years ago, some Protestant folk from Lurgan came and asked if I would start up a youth project for the YMCA. Lurgan is a very polarised community, divided evenly between Protestant and Catholic. The YMCA had been established for eight years at the top of the main street and they asked me if I would start the new venture at the bottom of the street. That's beyond the public toilets – they are the dividing line, the border line, believe it or not! I said to them, 'No problem, but I've no paper qualifications. All I have is my experience of life and of working with young people. The only One who has taught me is God Himself. I've nothing else to offer.' 'No better qual-ifications!' one man said, 'We'll go for it!'

So they gave me a building in the back of Shankill Parish, which I called 'The Well'. Bit by bit we started to build a place where the kids could come and feel secure. Whatever was going on in their lives outside, they could come in to The Well, whether they were Catholic or Protestant, in the knowledge that they would be looked after. The Well is a drop-in centre during the day and in the evening there is a more structured programme of Bible study, sport, dancing, drama and music. On Thursday evenings they have their own prayer group. It's the only place in the whole of Lurgan where Catholics and Protestants pray together. One of the group is a Presbyterian girl, Barbara, who gave me a lot of stick at the beginning, asking how we Catholics could be Christians. Now she's one of our strongest members – God opened her heart. She experienced in The Well that Jesus is alive and active and she experienced His love there. No matter how tough the kids are or where they come from, The Well's all about love. This is my life. It's the love of God that has me there, and it's His love that is turning around the lives of many young people, even as it has turned around mine.

28

MURDERED
ON THE WAY TO CHURCH

BERNADETTE POWER

*Bernadette's husband was shot dead in front of her and
her three young children. She testifies powerfully to how
Jesus helped her to forgive the Loyalist assassins and
pick up the pieces of her life.*

I was born into a Catholic family of eight children. My
father had a faith that he held to in his own unorthodox
way. Although he didn't speak about having a relationship with Jesus, he had great human relationships and he
brought us up in a disciplined yet loving family. We
didn't categorise people as Protestant or Catholic. That
was not part of our upbringing. He instilled in us a
respect for other people, especially older people. He was
a good man. He was only forty-one when he died suddenly of a brain tumour, leaving my mother with the
eight children, the oldest of whom was about seventeen.
She had a lot to cope with and life was hard for her. The
years that followed my father's death have few happy
memories for me.

I certainly didn't have a relationship with Jesus then.
I went to Mass, but I didn't know anything about
Christianity.

In my teenage years, the Troubles started and things
were very bad where I lived. Our family unit was breaking down, in a society that was also disintegrating. I

remember once, when I was about thirteen, standing in the porch of the church watching a family coming to evening Mass, the parents surrounded by their many children. I remember making an earnest prayer to God, 'I would love to be able just to talk to that family.' It's amazing how God answers prayer. I ended up marrying the eldest boy of that family, Mickey Power.

My whole life revolved around Mickey. He was my security. I constantly sought his attention and his affirmation of love, and he did not disappoint me. I thank God for my relationship with Mickey. It was through his love that I gradually grew in self-esteem and self-confidence.

One night I went to chapel and listened to a lovely girl, Christine McKay, whose husband had been shot in the driveway of her home. She had nursed him as he died in her arms. She spoke about the strength and the power of God in her life. I couldn't understand how this girl could have such forgiveness. Nothing would convince me that any power could enable a person to forgive such a thing. Yet, she made me think. God was trying to get a channel of grace into my life.

After that girl's testimony, I felt that somehow God was wanting to draw me closer to Himself. I went away on a weekend retreat – really it was an excuse to get away from the kids for a while and to relax with my friends. But as I sat in a church listening to a nun sharing about the passion of Christ, I remember closing my eyes and seeing this picture in my mind of a man and a boulder. Someone was pushing the boulder towards him and I was wondering who it was. Then I saw it was myself. I was rolling the boulder towards the Lord.

I opened my eyes and looked towards the altar. I felt burdened with all the resentment I had in my heart towards my own family and towards my husband's family. Low self-esteem was an added weight, pressing me down. Suddenly, I saw a vision of the Lord before me. I tried to snap out of it, thinking I must be moving towards a nervous breakdown. But the power of God touched me. It was as if, for a moment, God's Spirit and mine came together, as if the Lord Himself embraced me. I felt overcome. I was broken. But I know that I encountered the Lord personally and I remember saying in the church, 'Lord, I didn't know You. I didn't know.' I wept and wept. For three days afterwards, I was in physical pain. I remember saying, 'I believe. I believe that You are Jesus Christ. I believe that You're the Lord and I will go anywhere, Lord, for You. I'll go to the Shankill, Lord, I'll go to the Falls – wherever You want to send me, I'll go.' Coming away from there, the only thing I can say is that I fell in love with Jesus.

This was the beginning of my inner healing. The experience of the love of God drew me out from under the crushing pain of self-rejection, out of the loneliness of living apart from God, which is a desolation. I knew now that He loved me, though there was a hard journey in faith ahead of me.

I remember going to the priest and telling him what happened to me in the church. I said, 'I encountered the Lord here today! I encountered Jesus! He's alive!' He couldn't understand me.

When I came home and told Mickey what had happened, he was a wee bit stunned. I remember him saying to me, 'God love you, you've great faith. I haven't got faith like that.' Then one day we went together to hear someone giving a testimony and as we came away I said, 'Now, what did you think of that for a testimony to the power of God?' And Mickey said to me, 'I am going to pray and fast. I'm going to fast and ask that God would let me know Him. Maybe He's there, maybe He's not. I don't know.' So he prayed and fasted three days a week. He wanted a relationship with God. Through time, he came into a wonderful relationship with the Lord, and the two of us were blessed together and together we moved on in the knowledge of God. In places like the Christian Renewal Centre in Rostrevor, we met with lots of Christians from other denominations, and recognised in them our brothers and sisters in Christ.

Looking back now, I can see that, as I was growing in faith, the Lord was preparing me for the suffering that lay ahead. It came out of the blue one Sunday morning. Mickey was a taxi driver and had been working late the night before. I told him to stay at home and have a rest and I would go on to Mass with the children; he could go to a later Mass. I remember Mickey saying to me, 'No. We'll go and pray together, as a family.' We were in the car with the three children, the youngest of whom, Emma, was just eleven weeks old, when a gunman drew alongside and opened fire. Mickey was shot dead beside me. Michelle, whose eighth birthday was that week, was shot in the eye. Five-year-old Gavin was shot in the thigh.

Our whole world was blown to pieces. Michelle had to have eye surgery. Miraculously, her sight was saved, but she had to stay for some time in intensive care. Her whole face was lacerated, she had lead in her skull and she was opened along the hairline. Some glass remained in the back of her eye, because the operation to remove it would have been too risky. She can sometimes feel it moving about. There are also still fragments of lead lodged somewhere in her skull. Gavin had lead in his thigh and, ten days after the operation to remove it, his leg turned septic and he had to have the district nurse attend him at home for a further fortnight, to change his dressings.

My own wound could not be dressed. There I was, with Michelle recovering from surgery in the hospital, Gavin suffering at home, a little baby to care for, and my husband, the love of my life, brutally taken away from me. For me, there is no way a human being's faith endures that, other than through the power of God. I stood right at the foot of the cross, because there was nowhere else to go. Lots of people came with sympathy and good wishes, and then moved on in their own lives.

I was left to rear the children, to be there on my own. Now I had to walk in real faith. And, to be honest, in the earlier years, there wasn't a great deal of support. There were a lot of broken times when I felt I wasn't going to make it. At the worst of times, I would phone to Rostrevor and ask them if I could come down. There I felt that I was getting nourished by other faith friends in prayer. I would feel strengthened after a couple of days rest down in that house. I felt I could move on for another while in my own life with the children.

So for ten years I struggled. Many's the time the Lord consoled me in my desolation, but the reality is that for a long time I kicked doors in an agony of despair, I sat on the floor and cried day in and day out. I didn't draw the curtains, I didn't light a fire, I didn't put a bit of heat round the house. It wasn't pleasant for my children. There was a lot of pain, and yet we were together. We would go to the graveyard in the frost and snow and stay there till it grew dark. Nobody knew of all those darker times of brokenness, of what the three children had to go through, because their mother was broken. Because whatever I went through, they went through too. And yet those three children have gone on to have their own personal relationship with the Lord. And now, ten years down the line, I am looking for a resurrection period. I still have the hurt, of course, it's still constantly being healed. I still have times of longing that their childhood could have been more uplifting and more blessed, more pleasant for them. But the fact is that they had a lot of suffering.

Many a time, I lost my head and in my humanity cursed and swore because I was so broken – nothing but a sinner wrecked and broken and in desolation. But in the midst of all that, there was still the firm acknowledgement that I knew in my heart that Jesus hadn't walked away. Everybody else had walked away, but He didn't. And there were times when the Lord did send a faith friend to come and help carry the load. I remember

Christmas time was a very painful time and I could not get my head round sitting in the house alone with three children on Christmas Day. I even resented the fact that the Lord had the crucifixion over a weekend. I'd have it out with Him, up front and honest. 'Let me tell You something! I'm in it for years here. At least Your crucifixion was over in a day but mine's still continuing. Struggling, with three babies and a house broken and falling down round me. With desolation in my heart . . .' I know that's pathetic, but that was the reality. You have to acknowledge your pain and the ugliness of it, with no light in it. I still knew He was there. I didn't blame Him for Mickey being murdered, because even in the lowest of times I still knew that God didn't sanction that. It was sin in somebody else's life – it was a work of darkness inspired by Satan. It was the darkness that moved in to take Mickey's life, to rob us of our marriage, to rob my children of their father. Such deeds are done in this country.

Mickey would have known lots of ex-UVF guys who had been converted. Some of them were great friends of his. Some had been brought to realise that they were walking in darkness through Mickey talking with them. I've never seen the face of the man that murdered Mickey. I don't believe he was ever arrested for it. But I would still pray and say, 'Lord, whoever he is, show him the mercy that You've shown me.' That's my prayer. I could never say that I know what forgiveness means. All I know is that, in faith, my prayer is, 'Lord if he goes before You, have mercy on him.'

In the journey of faith, I believe that the Lord is always challenging us to change, to leave off the old, to put on the new. Daily I ask, 'Lord what is the new for today?' He says things like 'Bernadette, go back to the kids and say "I was wrong" '. So I go back and affirm my children. And constantly I pray as well, 'Lord place me where You want me to be. Help me to discern, in my life, where You want me to go, and what you want me to do.'

The Lord is directing my life. For the moment, my priority is to be with my three children, trying to raise them with an awareness of who they are, they are individuals, unique and different. I want to help them to know their strengths and draw them out, to encourage them in any weaknesses they may have and to love them. I am blessed to have them.

I believe that in whatever we are called to do, should it be sitting nursing a child with a wounded knee, should it be drying somebody's runny nose, that is holiness.

I know if Christ my Lord had not somehow upheld me, I could not have emerged from this onslaught of evil. Yet His grace has proved sufficient for me and for my children. I'm just an ordinary human being with very little education. But I know something the world could never teach me. I know that my Redeemer lives and that in all things He works for the good of those who love Him (Romans 8:28)..

29

REJOICE IN THE LORD ALWAYS
REV PAUL SYMONDS

Paul is a Catholic Curate in South Belfast, involved with the United Prayer Breakfast and in various reconciliation projects in Northern Ireland.

My parents were nominal Anglicans. Both had been baptised, but neither had been confirmed, nor ever received Holy Communion. They rarely went to church. They would have called themselves 'Christians' from a moral, rather than a spiritual perspective. Throughout their lives they lived as good, honest citizens and tried, from my earliest age, to instil values of honesty and integrity in me. God and prayer did have a place in their lives, though, and one of my earliest memories is of my mother sitting me on the kitchen table and teaching me the Lord's prayer. As they grew older they became increasingly open to the spiritual dimension of life and, after my father's death, my mother became a Catholic, mainly because she experienced such positive support from her Catholic friends and recognised that they drew their strength from communion with Christ in the Eucharist.

I was very close to my grandmothers, both of whom were women of deep faith and personal love of God. My mother's mother never went to church, but she had a deep prayer life and taught me from a very early age to appreciate her simple, intercessory style of prayer. She also had a picture book about Jesus, which I used to love to read. On the day I was born, she gave me a little Authorised Version of the Bible and a Book of Common

Prayer of the Church of England. They are treasured pos-
sessions. The print is so small I can hardly read it now,
but the Bible is well thumbed from assiduous reading
when I was younger, before I discovered the more modern translations. My maternal grandmother had had a
hard life, but she radiated the love of God and the peace
that passes all understanding and I adored her until she
died at the age of ninety-one, when I was about eighteen.

My father's mother was a little younger and still lived
in the house in London where my father had grown up.
I used to enjoy spending holidays with her when I was a
teenager. She, too, had a deep faith in God. She did not
belong to any particular church, but she attended
services in different churches, insisting that they all worshipped the same Father of our Lord Jesus Christ and
that the Catholic Church was the Mother Church of all
the others. She strongly disapproved of 'Bonfire Night'
on 5th November, because she said it was anti-Catholic.
It was years before I read the story of Guy Fawkes and
understood what she meant.

When I was five, I was sent to school at the Marist
Convent, a short walk down the road from the back of
our house. The Church of England primary school was in
the High Street, just opposite my parents' shop, but, for
reasons I've never really fathomed, they opted for the
Catholic school. The Marist Sisters had moved to our village just two years earlier, because their convent in
London had been bombed during the war. I was bliss-
fully happy at my convent primary school. Practically all
the teachers were nuns, mostly very young and mostly
from the West of Ireland. The make-up of the school was
about sixty per cent Protestant or non-denominational
and about forty per cent Catholic. The nuns opened up
the Bible to me and I was fascinated by the accounts in
the Old Testament of the patriarchs and the prophets, the
Exodus and the crossing of the Red Sea. But most of all
the nuns helped me to deepen my knowledge and love
of the Lord Jesus, whom I already knew slightly from my

grandmother's 'Jesus book'. The nuns radiated joy and
the love of God and when they spoke of the Lord Jesus it
was obvious that they were speaking not of a man who'd
lived 2,000 years ago, but of a Saviour who was alive and
present here and now!

Reverend Mother, as we called her in those days, was
an English woman. Years later, when I was a university
student, we became close friends. I then understood how
her deep personal faith and intimate knowledge and
love of the Lord Jesus had permeated the whole convent
and so influenced my early formation. She showed me,
by example, how the love of Jesus transcends all denominational boundaries. She herself had many Christian
friends of other denominations and certainly, as children,
we would have been taught by the nuns to have a great
respect for all the Churches. Indeed, I wouldn't have
thought in terms of denomination and, whilst at primary
school, I also enjoyed warm friendship with the local
Anglican curate and his family, who lived just opposite
the convent. When asked once by a girl from the senior
school if I were a Catholic or a Protestant, I answered in
all honesty 'I don't know!'

My parents were married in a Methodist church in
London and, when I came along, they had me baptised
in the same church. They liked the simplicity of
Methodist worship. All the main Churches which prac-
tise infant baptism recognise the validity of each other's
baptism. From my experience, I have always believed
that in my baptism in the Methodist Church I received
the gift of new life and the Holy Spirit, which enabled me
to respond with faith when I heard the gospel preached
in my Catholic primary school. The headmaster of
Windsor Grammar School, where I did my secondary
education, was a Methodist and a devout man. He put
great emphasis on the quality of worship in morning
assembly and in many ways nourished my personal
faith, for I very rarely attended church during my school
days, though I frequently went into churches, Catholic or

Anglican, to pray on my own.

French was always my favourite subject at school and I greatly looked forward to going to university to read it, with a view to becoming a teacher. Throughout my primary school I'd wanted to be a priest, but that fell into abeyance during my grammar school years. I won an open scholarship in French to St David's College, Lampeter. Lampeter had been established jointly by Oxford and Cambridge in 1822 as a place for Welsh ordinands to study without leaving their native Wales. It was like an Oxbridge college in the middle of the Welsh hills. By the late 1960s it had become a university college open to anyone, but there was still a vibrant Anglican tradition there. I started attending Evensong, which was a very positive experience of the beauty of Anglican worship. All my friends were believers, of various denominations, and many of them were intending to take Holy Orders in the Anglican Church. I envied the commitment of my Christian friends and my latent vocation to the priesthood re-surfaced.

During the Christmas holidays of my first year at university, I went to visit the Marist Sisters in my old primary school. I spent an afternoon talking to the various sisters who had taught me. As I walked home down the long, tree-lined drive of the convent, I was suddenly overwhelmed with a sense of joy flooding my whole being and the conviction that Christ had chosen me to follow Him as a priest. I'd had a similar experience about ten months earlier in Notre Dame cathedral in Paris, when I was there thinking about my maternal grandmother who had died a few weeks before. Years later, I came to recognise that joy as an encounter with the Holy Spirit, an empowering which was like being born again. I had another very similar experience on Ascension Day 1989, in a little retreat house called Palazzola, just outside Rome, when I felt the Lord choosing me and calling me to follow Him in Northern Ireland. And yet again in May 1991, on the feast of St Matthias, in the same chapel

of Palazzola, when I felt the Lord calling me to seek
admission to the Diocese of Down & Connor and give
my whole life to him in Northern Ireland. On that occasion, the sense of being chosen was quite overwhelming.

All my life I've had friends in various Christian
denominations. I have a special love of the Anglican tradition and I feel very much at home in the Church of
Ireland. But I am also very comfortable worshipping in
Presbyterian, Methodist and Baptist churches. It was
said of my paternal grandmother that 'she could take her
place in anyone's sitting room'. I like to feel that I could
take my place in a wide variety of Christian places of
worship. But I believe that commitment to Christ also
demands commitment to follow Him in a specific, living
tradition. It was in the Catholic Church that I first met
the living Lord Jesus and I believe that it is in the
Catholic Church that Christ called me to follow Him.
Since the Second Vatican Council, ecumenism, or the
pursuit of the re-union in Christ of all the Churches, has
been an essential part of Catholic spirituality. I believe
that Christ has given me particular gifts to help in that
area. I rejoice in and draw strength from my fellowship
with all who are in Christ, both in my own tradition and
in the other traditions in which I am privileged to share.
The doctrine of the communion of saints, asserted in the
Apostles' Creed, is very important to me. I see ecumenism as first and foremost the sharing of gifts.

The Catholic Church, like every other living Christian
tradition, is in constant need of renewal and purification,
though not every change is prompted by the Holy Spirit,
which is why we need to take seriously the words of
Paul to the Thessalonians: 'Test everything. Hold on to
the good' (1 Thessalonians 5:21). The same advice
applies to expressions of prayer and devotion. Not every
form of spirituality embraced by the Catholic Church
appeals to me. However, I do find my faith perfectly mirrored in the creeds, the writings of the early Church
Fathers, the teachings of the Second Vatican Council and

most of all in the liturgy of the Church: the Liturgy of the Hours, made up of psalms and Scripture readings and sanctifying the different times of the day. My faith is also mirrored in the Liturgy of the Eucharist, in which the proclamation of the Word of God and the prayer of thanksgiving constantly recall God's saving work throughout history, culminating in the unique, all-sufficient sacrifice of Jesus Christ on the cross and the outpouring of the Holy Spirit.

From my earliest youth I have found in the liturgy of the Catholic Church a powerful encounter with the risen Lord Jesus – a privileged encounter to which I look forward with eager anticipation every day. For me, the liturgy expresses the truth of my favourite words of Scripture, written by Paul to the Philippians:

Rejoice in the Lord always. I will say it again: Rejoice! Let your gentleness be evident to all. The Lord is near. Do not be anxious about anything, but in everything, by prayer and petition, with thanksgiving, present your requests to God. And the peace of God, which transcends all understanding, will guard your hearts and your minds in Christ Jesus (4:4–7).

APPENDIX I

WHAT IS AN EVANGELICAL CATHOLIC?

Millions of Roman Catholics throughout the world have a personal relationship with Jesus, many of them through the various Renewal Movements in the Catholic Church. They are evangelical in the strictest sense of the term, in that they have received the basic gospel, accepted Jesus as personal Lord and Saviour and are manifesting the fruit of the Holy Spirit in their daily lives.

These 'Evangelical Catholics' have a growing love and respect for Scripture as the Word of God. They are born again Christians. They would identify themselves variously as committed Christians, Charismatic Catholics, renewed Catholics, born again Catholics, or simply Catholics who love the Lord. Surely they are brothers and sisters in Christ of all evangelical Christians in the various Protestant Churches.

Evangelical Catholics affirm:

† That salvation cannot be earned, it is a free gift – however, the evidence of good deeds indicating that one has become a committed Christian must then follow.

† That there is only one mediator between God and men, the person of Jesus Christ (1 Tim 2:5).

† The priesthood of all believers, which means that a Christian has direct access to the Father through Jesus.

† That Scripture in its entirety (both Old and New Testaments) is the inspired authoritative Word of God.

† That the Eucharist (or Mass) is not a repetition of

Calvary. Jesus died once and for all. The priest and people enter into that one all-sufficient sacrifice by Grace.

† Heaven for those who accept the salvation won by Jesus
and hell for those who die unrepentant for their wicked-
ness.

† That all human beings are born into a state of separation
from God as a result of the Fall.

† That Jesus died on the cross in atonement for all sin, and
that in His death, He took the place of all sinners in bearing their guilt (Isaiah 53:6).

† That Jesus will come again in glory to judge the living
and the dead.

Note: The above affirmations are part of the official teaching of
the Roman Catholic Church, being found in the *Decree on the
Laity* (Chapter 2), *Dogmatic Constitution on the Church* (Chapters
2 &7), *Dogmatic Constitution on Divine Revelation* (Chapters 1, 3,
4), and *Constitution on Sacred Liturgy* (Chapter 1).

Evangelical Catholics would subscribe to the tenets of the
Lausanne Covenant (1974). This includes the 'confessions' in
the Covenant: *'We confess that we have often denied our calling . . .
have compromised our message, manipulated our hearers . . .'* It is
important to note that the tenets of the Lausanne Covenant are
not at variance with the official teaching of the Catholic
Church.

Evangelical Catholics believe that:

1. The Roman Catholic Church is a Christian Church that
has taken on some un-Christian practices over the centuries. However a major renewal of the Holy Spirit has
been and is taking place, directly as a result of the Second
Vatican Council addressing these issues.

2. The Holy Spirit is moving to bring both renewal and
revival in the Roman Catholic Church as in other
Christian Churches.

3. Many members of the Roman Catholic Church, while

being perhaps over-sacramentalised, have been under-evangelised and therefore its members need to be called, as adults, to accept Jesus as personal Lord and Saviour. In the words of Pope Paul VI in his Encyclical on Evangelization: *'The Church exists in order to evangelize . . . she begins by first being evangelized herself.'*

4. There are many God-made traditions in the Roman Catholic Church which will stand the test of time.

The Roman Catholic Church affirms the historic doctrine of the Nicene Creed (the virgin birth, bodily resurrection of Jesus, etc.). Every Catholic Christian is asked to affirm this Creed every time they participate in the celebration of the Sunday Eucharist (Mass).

Evangelical Catholics are committed to:

• Jesus as the only way to Salvation – one day every knee shall bow and every tongue confess that Jesus Christ is truly Lord.

• The necessity of the empowering of the Holy Spirit for the committed Christian to achieve his/her full potential and do the works of Christ.

• The priority of evangelism (see below*) within the life of the local Catholic Church, as well as a commitment to join with committed Christians in other denominations in the fulfilment of the biblical command to take Christ to all the nations.

• A respect for and obedience to the teaching authority of the Pope and Bishops of the Catholic Church, unless that obedience goes against one's conscience as enlightened by Scripture and Church teaching.

* An excellent definition of evangelism has been produced by the Evangelisation 2000 Office in Rome:

– To proclaim with the Power of the Holy Spirit (Acts 1:8)
– The Incarnate, Crucified, Resurrected and Living Jesus

Christ (Acts 2:32)
- As the only Saviour (Acts 4:12)
- And Divine Lord (Philippians 2:9–11)
- Of all mankind (1 Timothy 2:4; 4.10; Titus 2:11)
- And of the whole person (Ephesians 1:22–23)
- In a joyful, loving and effective way
- That contributes to building the Church (Colossians 1:18–23)
- By making Jesus known, loved, honoured, followed and obeyed to the ends of the earth (Matthew 28:19)

Published by Fr. Aidan Carroll, Joe Dalton, Jim Donnan, Monsignor Tom Fehily, Larry Hogan, Fr. Frank Hyland, Ronan Johnston, Fr. Padraig McCarthy, Morgan McStay, John Manning, Paddy Monaghan, Joe O' Sullivan, Barry Reynolds, Ann Riordan, Jim Sherlock (Dublin); Jerry Carbery (Athy); Maura Devine (Carlow); Tadg Dwyer (Cork); Dennis O'Brien (Laois); Peter O'Sullivan (Dundalk); Michael Frawley (Galway); Michael McKenna (Letterkenny); Edward Stone (Ballinasloe); David Blake, Fr. Noel Burke (Limerick); Fr. Matt Cunningham (Tipperary); George McAuliffe (Tralee); Al Ryan (Waterford); Fr Jim Cogley (Wexford); Mary Smith (Monaghan); Ed Conlin, Fr. Brendan Murray, Fr. John Murray, Fr. Ciaran Dallat (Belfast); Fr. Neal Carlin (Derry); Sr. Monica Cavanagh (Portadown); Eugene Boyle (Rostrevor); Fr. Pat Lynch (Birmingham); Cormac O'Duffy (Coventry); Fr Ronnie Mitchel (Glasgow); Kees Slijkerman (The Netherlands); Philip Maloney (Australia); Keith Fournier (USA); Sr Catherine Casey (Jerusalem).

© 'With Ecclesiastical Permission, Dublin November 1990.'

Background notes on 'What is an Evangelical Catholic?'

Purpose of Document

A number of Catholic lay leaders and clergy drew up this document as one contribution to this Decade of Evangelism. It is a straightforward and clear statement of Catholic Christianity, with an evangelical emphasis. Part of its purpose is to foster genuine evangelism, while avoiding proselytism.

The intention is not to produce a definitive theological

statement on all aspects of Catholic belief, such as sacrament, ministry and authority, so much as a relatively simple definition of some fundamental beliefs that will, hopefully, facilitate dialogue and co-operation in evangelism.

The **aim is** to focus attention on those areas that are central to the life of every Catholic Christian and thus remove some of the barriers to Christians working together, which often derive from wrong perceptions of Catholic Church teaching on the Mass, the role of Mary, salvation, etc. Accordingly, this document states that Christians in the Roman Catholic Church believe

'. . . that salvation cannot be earned, it is a free gift'

'. . . that there is only one mediator between God and man, the person Jesus Christ'

'. . . that the Eucharist (or Mass) is not a repetition of Calvary'.

Evangelical Catholics also hold that a commitment to caring for the poor, the sick and the disadvantaged is an integral element in a commitment to evangelism.

What does Evangelical mean?

The word Evangelical has been misunderstood and disowned by Catholics because of its association with the Protestant Churches and with fundamentalism. However, the word actually originates from the Greek word for gospel in the New Testament (*euaggelion*) and describes those whose lives have been transformed by the message of the gospel, which they now seek to proclaim by word and deed.

This emphasis on proclaiming the 'Good News' was highlighted by the Vatican Council and subsequently by Pope Paul VI, who stated, in his Encyclical *'Evangelii Nuntiandi'* (Evangelisation In the Modern World) that it was to be the Catholic Church's central mission.

Decade of Evangelism

In his Encyclical *'Redemptoris Missio'*, issued in 1991, Pope John Paul II stated that 'God is preparing a great springtime for Christianity'. He called for a full commitment of all Catholics to a new evangelisation in this Decade of Evangelism, declaring:

'I sense the moment has come to commit all of the Church's ener-

gies to a new evangelisation. No believer in Christ, no institution
of the Church can avoid this supreme duty – to proclaim Christ to
all peoples.'

This has been given practical expression in the establishment of
the Evangelisation 2000 Office in Rome (whose purpose is to
promote this 'Decade of Evangelism'), as well as through many
renewal movements within the Catholic Church, e.g.,
Charismatic Renewal, Cursillo, Christian Family Movement,
Focolare, Oasis, etc., all of which emphasise the necessity for
Catholics to make a personal commitment, as adults, to Jesus
Christ as Lord and Saviour.

The primary objectives of this Decade of Evangelism are
that fifty per cent or more of the world's population might be
Christian by the end of the decade, and that the existing
Christian Churches might be renewed. This is surely impossible without Christians learning to work together in evangelism
and associated areas, e.g. rehabilitation programmes, pro-life
agencies, etc.

Appendix II

WHY YOU NEED TO READ THE BIBLE

1. Because it is God's inspired Word

Vatican Council states that 'All Scripture (both Old and New Testament) is inspired by God and useful for teaching, for reproving, for correcting, for instruction in justice that the man of God may be perfect, equipped for every good work'. (Dogmatic Constitution on Divine Revelation, Section 11. Also 2 Timothy 3:16 & 17)

In encouraging us not to neglect reading the Old Testament as well as the New, Vatican Council states that 'God, the inspirer and author of both testaments, wisely arranged that the New Testament be hidden in the Old and the Old be made manifest in the New . . . The books of the Old Testament with all their parts . . . acquire and show forth their full meaning in the New Testament and in turn shed light on it and explain it'. (Decree on Divine Revelation, Section 16)

2. Because the Bible is true and essential for today as always

That's why Vatican Council states that 'The books of Scripture must be acknowledged as teaching firmly, faithfully and **without error** that truth which God wanted put into the sacred writings for the sake of our salvation'. (Dogmatic Constitution on Divine Revelation, Section 11)

3. Because Jesus said:

'Man shall not live by bread alone, but by every word that proceeds from the mouth of God' (Matthew 4:4).

4. Because it shows the way you can have a personal relationship with God

Vatican Council specifically asks all Christians to read the Bible frequently in order to **know** Jesus.

'This sacred Synod earnestly and specifically urges all the Christian faithful to learn by frequent reading of   the divine Scriptures the excelling knowledge of Jesus Christ. For ignorance of the Scriptures is ignorance of Christ . . . And let them remember that prayer should accompany the reading of sacred Scripture, so that God and man may talk together.' (Dogmatic Constitution on Divine Revelation Section 25)

Jesus Himself said:'
'And this is eternal life that they know thee the only true God and Jesus Christ whom thou has sent' (John 17:3).

If you do not have a personal relationship with God, then ask Jesus to take over your life and be your personal Saviour and Lord. He will transform your life and bring meaning where there was emptiness.

5. Because it challenges us to spread the Good News of salvation

Jesus said to His disciples:
'Go into all the world and preach the Gospel to the whole creation. He who believes and is baptised will be saved, but he who does not believe will be condemned' (Mark 16:15–16).

Vatican Council states what the primary duty of a priest is:
'Since no one can be saved who has not first believed, priests have as their primary duty the proclamation of the Gospel of God to all . . . For through the saving Word, the spark of faith is struck in the hearts of unbelievers and fed in the hearts of the faithful.' (Decree on the Ministry of Priests, Section 4)
Let us encourage our priests and ministers and pray that they will be filled with the Holy Spirit as they fulfil their primary duty of proclaiming the Gospel.

This command of Jesus is not to be obeyed only by priests and ministers, but by all Christian lay people, as we allow the Holy Spirit to empower us for this task.

Vatican Council affirmed this when it stated that all

Christian lay people should 'look for opportunities to announce Christ by words addressed either to non-believers with a view to leading them to faith or to believers (both Catholic and Protestant) with a view to instructing and strengthening them and motivating them toward a more fervant life'. (Decree on Laity, Section 6)

6. The way to forgiveness

'If we confess our sins, he is faithful and just and will forgive our sins and cleanse us from all unrighteousness (1 John 1:9).

'For Christ also died for sins once for all, the righteous for the unrighteous, that he might bring us to God' (1 Peter 3:18).

7. God's plan for salvation

'For God so loved the world that he gave his only Son, that whoever believes in him [Jesus] should not perish but have eternal life' (John 3:16).

'I am the Way and the Truth and the Life; no one comes to the Father, but by me' (John 14:6).

8. How to overcome temptation

'Submit yourselves therefore to God, resist the devil and he will flee from you' (James 4:7).

9. Purity

'How can a young man keep his way pure? By guarding it according to thy word' (Psalm 119:9).

10. Direction for life

'Thy word is a lamp to my feet and a light to my path' (Psalm 119:105).

Appendix III

LIFE-CHANGING CHALLENGE

Although we may have been baptised as infants at the behest of our parents or godparents, nevertheless, every one of us must make the decision to surrender his or her life totally and completely to Jesus. Yielding your life to Jesus enables you to face the following crucial questions with peace in your heart: *If you were to die right now, do you know where you would spend eternity? Will you be with God forever in Heaven? Does Jesus live within you through His Holy Spirit?*

If you are unsure, here are four things for you to do immediately:

1. **Put all your trust in Jeus Christ, who died to save you from your sins.**

2. **Admit that you are a sinner and, in sincere repentance, ask God to forgive your sins through Jesus' sacrifice on Calvary.**

3. **Make Jesus Lord of your life. Invite Him into your contrite heart to be in control of your life and your destiny. Accept Jesus Christ as Lord and Saviour of your own life and become a completely new creature in Him.**
If you have never sincerely and genuinely made that commitment of your life to Jesus, then why not do so now with this simple prayer:

Heavenly Father, I come before you in Jesus' Name. I am truly sorry for my sins and I confess with my mouth and believe in my heart that Jesus died and paid the price for my sins on Calvary, was buried and was raised from the dead on the third day. I ask you to forgive all my

sins and to come and live in my heart. I ask you to empower me now
with your Holy Spirit. Thank you, Lord. Amen.

It was St Leo the Great who reminded us that nobody is refused
because of sin, because to be born again and reconciled with
God is not something to be earned (or learned). It is a gift of
God through the Blood of Christ.

If you have sincerely prayed this prayer, this is truly the
first day of the rest of your life! Rejoice and be glad in it.

4. Now tell someone else what you have done.
Jesus said: *'So if anyone declares himself for me in the presence of
men, I will declare myself for him in the presence of my Father in
heaven'* (Matthew 10:32).

You may be attacked by doubts about the reality and purpose
of the decision you have made. If this occurs, above all, remember this: *'God has called you and he will not fail you.'*
(1 Thessalonians 5:24)

Now that you have committed your life to Christ, begin to read
the Scriptures daily, join a prayer group or Bible Study and
become active in the life of your local church. Some helpful
daily Bible reading notes, available from Christian bookshops,
are: Bible Alive, The Word Among Us, The Word for Today,
Every Day With Jesus or Daily Light. You might also consider
doing an Alpha Bible Study Course or a Life in the Spirit
Seminar.

God is faithful and He can indeed be trusted to finish the work
which He has begun in you. If you have now made this
momentous decision, please write to us and let us know. We
want to share in your joy. Write to: Evangelical Catholic
Initiative at **either** 7 Northumberland Ave., Dun Laoghaire, Co.
Dublin, Rep. of Ireland **or** Mizpah, Forest Drive, Shore Rd.,
Rostrevor, Co. Down BT34 3AA, N. Ireland.